Brenda Mallon is an inspirational therapist and trainer whose workshops on creative visualizations and personal development have been a transformational experience for thousands of people. For over 16 years, her wise and compassionate approach in seminars, courses and in one-to-one work has proved to be the key to making significant life changes. She is the author of several books on dreaming, counselling and positive strategies for renewal and growth.

Creative Visualization with Colour

Healing Your Life with the
Power of Colour

Brenda Mallon

vega

First published by Element Books Ltd 1999

ISBN 1-84333-156-X

A catalogue record for this book is available from the British Library

Published in 2002 by
Vega
64 Brewery Road
London, N7 9NT

A member of Chrysalis Books plc

Visit our website at www.chrysalisbooks.co.uk

Printed in Great Britain
by Lightning Source
Cover designed by Design Revolution, Brighton

Contents

Acknowledgements viii

Introduction ix

1 Mapmakers' Colours 1

2 Red: Warming the Heart 27

3 Feeling Blue 42

4 The Green Light 57

5 Yellow: Sunshine for Sensuous Success 71

6 Power of Purple 85

7 The Shadows with Silver Linings 96

8 Tones of Tranquillity 107

9 The Rainbow of Radiance 116

10 Sifting for Gold 124

Further Reading 144

Useful Addresses 146

Index 148

for Zoot Joe Aladdin Mallon:
a rainbow maker

Acknowledgements

The opportunity to say thank you to all those who have helped throughout the writing of this book starts with the clients who have shared their creativity and visions with me. Though you remain unnamed, know that our journey together has been life affirming and my gratitude is heartfelt.

My thanks and love to Wendy Macdonald, Tim Wallbank, Dave Burnham and Linda Drury for long walks and new ways of seeing the world; Margaret Warbrick for her generosity and insights about Aura-Soma; Judi Ledward for always being such a good listener; Miranda Tufnell for sharing her powerful honesty and originality in the field of creativity; Callum Thomas for his knowledge of colour codes in the natural world; Ken Newton for his theories about beige; Jeannie Civil for being such a great colleague and friend who gives unstintingly.

Special gratitude to Grace Cheetham, my editor at Element, for her guidance, clarity, vision and constant support.

Thanks to my children Karl, Crystal and Daniel, who each add rich colour to my life in their own individual ways. And finally, a huge thank you to Styx, for believing, for giving time and for being here.

Introduction

This book shows how you can use colour and creative visualization to improve your life in every way. It offers straightforward, easily understood techniques that can enhance your relationships, improve your health and prosperity, and heal past hurts. I know creative visualization with colour works because I use it in my work with people suffering from anxiety and depression, with others who lack confidence and cannot achieve their goals in work or in relationships, with corporate clients who face radical change in their careers, with clients who fear failure and with those who feel unhappy though they appear to have achieved everything materially they could ever have hoped for.

Creative Visualization with Colour addresses all of these areas – and more – and contains a whole range of ways in which you can strengthen your ability to get the most out of life. You are surrounded by colour every moment of every day and with this book you will learn how to creatively harness its vital power.

Within the book there are visualizations with specific colours to develop your intuition and spiritual awareness so that you can access your inner wisdom and discover personal healing space. The practical exercises in each chapter allow you to build up a repertoire of insights and affirmations which you then collect together in the final chapter in the form of a personal action plan. This will be a unique source of strength in times of challenge and an unfailing aid to your creativity.

When you have finished the book and sifted for gold in the final chapter, I would love to hear about your experiences. Feedback from readers is one of the great joys of being a writer. Contact me at 7 Didsbury Park, Didsbury, Manchester M20 5LH, England or email: lapwing@gn.apc.org

1

Mapmakers' Colours

Mapmakers' tints contain the most delicate and intense of all the colours, like those of the inspired artist; these colours describe the unknown territory of the world and reveal mysterious places to the uninitiated. *Creative Visualization with Colour* combines the eye for colour of the artist and the insight of the mapmaker to create a revolutionary new way of exploring intuitive wisdom and creativity. Your journey will be a voyage into aspects of the self you've not yet encountered – or maybe even dreamt of.

The powerful conjunction of 'colour' and 'creative visualization' will take you into a brand new world of positive potential and personal renewal. It is a unique, fluid, enabling process that will reveal your inner, intuitive knowledge. Using the practical techniques and visualizations in the book you will learn to increase your ability to find new ways of harnessing your creative powers for enhanced health, wealth and well-being. Your compassion, for both yourself and others will be strengthened and your sense of connection with the wholeness of life will find a new direction.

This first chapter is the compass that sets the points for your expedition; it includes a brief description of creative visualization and examples of its use, followed by the same for colour therapy, and from there we enter the unique domain of 'creative visualization with colour'.

Creative Visualization

Creativity is something we are all born with, yet this talent is often wasted through lack of use. *Creative Visualization with Colour* is your personal training guide to help you get in shape for your journey into the realms of your creative landscape – an experience which will be full of beauty, wonders and crystal-clear pools of insight.

You'll find that the more you exercise, develop and expand your creative mind, the more powerful it will become and your creative confidence will soar. No matter who or what you are or what your previous life experiences have been, you can begin your creative development programme now.

What is Creative Visualization?

Creative visualization is the process of harnessing the power of your mind using imagery to achieve a goal. It is positive thinking taken a great deal further and can be used for any part of your life, be it physical, emotional or spiritual. Visualization is not a form of hypnosis; it is a heightened state of relaxation which allows you to engage with the parts of your being normally hidden in the hectic activity that is the stuff of everyday life.

First you relax your body, then you let your mind rest. This does not mean that you have to make your mind completely blank, rather that you quieten it. The simplest way to understand this, if you have not done it before, is to imagine a clear blue sky. Next imagine a cloud coming along – you notice it but then you take your attention back to the blue of the sky and let the cloud drift away. Think of your quietened mind as the clear blue sky and the clouds that come along as thoughts that come into your mind which you acknowledge but do not concentrate on.

When you quieten your mind, alpha brain waves are produced and it is during this stage that your subconscious mind is capable of the most effective communication and reorganization. During this alpha period, you can directly influence both your physical responses and your mental state and by introducing chosen imagery you can begin to reprogramme less positive thinking so that you can move towards what it is you want to achieve. When you regularly imagine achieving an objective, you actually change. Your mind absorbs the subliminal messages and, in response, your attitude and behaviour alter. Instead of being driven by the subconscious mind, your hidden powerhouse, you can influence it positively.

This powerful technique combining innate intuition, imagination, cognitive processes and self-direction lets you uncover who you really are and what you are intended to be. Creative visualization lets you access the very special places within you to find meaningful direction and purpose.

It is a mental rehearsal for your best-ever performance so it is useful to end each visualization with a positive affirmation.

A SIMPLE EXPERIMENT

In order to give yourself an opportunity to discover the power of creative visualization I want you to try an experiment. Sit quietly and then imagine a lemon. Try to see the bright lemon skin, feel the shiny surface and then see yoursef cutting it in half. Can you imagine the juice on your fingertips? Now take up the lemon and smell its sharp aroma. Are your senses alert and reacting to this lemon even though it is not physically in front of you? Finally, squeeze some of the juice into your mouth. What has happened to your taste buds? Are they reacting as if you had actually bitten into a lemon? Is your saliva flowing? Did you screw up your eyes at the imagined bitterness?

If you had any of these sensations then you know that what you create in your mind can affect you physically. Creative visualization is as simple as that. It is about using all your senses to create a new vision in your mind, which in turn has a physical impact on your body.

When Was Creative Visualization First Used?

Among the earliest records of human beings there are paintings which reveal our magical imagination, possibly the greatest tool we possess. By depicting themselves in the skins of animals or drawing a successful hunt, these early ancestors show how the power of thought invokes success. And at that time it really was a matter of life and death – if they didn't catch their food they starved! This 'magical thinking', or 'sympathetic magic' as it is sometimes known, is harnessed in creative visualization.

Just as ancient man visualized his future, so can we, as we approach the millennium, by employing the same visualization tool. In our imaginations we can rehearse a successful outcome, we can change old negative patterns by seeing ourselves acting in positive, life-enhancing ways. We can accept that we can and do influence our lives.

The ancient Greeks believed that visualization enabled them to achieve their heart's desire. When a woman became pregnant she would be surrounded with beautiful objects – vases, flowers, carvings and the like – in the belief that everything she saw would influence her, both awake and asleep, and this in turn would affect the growing embryo. More recently, this belief has been validated by research which shows that pregnant women who listen to calming classical music give birth to babies who are calmer – the embryos have been filmed in utero responding to the music!

How Does Creative Visualization Work?

If you think how people are 'programmed' to behave in certain ways, for instance by education or social conditioning, you can see that with a different system they could have learnt very different skills. In our society, feelings of personal inadequacy are often the result of negative training or abusive life experiences. In some cases poor schooling undermines talent and punishes creativity by insisting that there is only one way to do things, or that the teacher always knows best.

The rise of personal trainers, motivational managers and sports psychologists has shown how psychological attitude affects performance. This is done by visualizing success and building up self-confidence through affirmations. Believe you can do something and you are more likely to prove you can.

Parental dreams and demands

Perhaps in your family what your parents demanded was what you had to deliver; for example, maybe you wanted to be an illustrator but they insisted you took an accountancy course. Sometimes parents insist on life paths for their children which fulfil their own unrealized ambitions rather than those which reflect the gifts of the child. At other times it happens because they are trying to protect the child from their own fears of failure, poverty or social isolation.

This influence also applies to many other aspects of life: the choice of marriage partner we make, the religious rituals we follow, where we choose to live and with whom, the friendships we make or break because of parental approval or disapproval, even the kind of clothes we wear. If this has happened to you then you will recognize how disempowering it can be.

Focus on the positive

The good news is that what you have learnt can be 'unlearnt'. Focusing on the positive can change your life, which is where visualization comes in. What you can do is use your imagination: you can bring the *image* of how you want to be in to your mind and replace those self-defeating ideas that limit your happiness. Creative visualization is a process which helps you preview goals, which in turn sets up conditions that make them achievable.

It has been proved that positive thoughts have positive outcomes. So think of happiness, joy, exuberance, fun and success and you will feel happy, energized and at ease with yourself and the world. If you think negatively and are judgemental, critical, pessimistic, resentful and fearful, you will feel tense, alienated, miserable and worn out. By using colour visualization techniques you can learn to accentuate the positive.

Powerful relaxation

Achieving a state of relaxation is a crucial stage of creative visualization: it allows your imagination to operate without the hindrance of the doubts and questions – the 'What ifs?' and 'How will Is?' that are common when we operate on a purely cognitive level. Relaxation reduces fear, and the tight rigidity that causes tension headaches and stiff necks is eased out as muscles soften in the warmth that seems to spread during a colour visualization session.

When we are fully relaxed we become more in tune with our inner selves. As the outer world with all its distractions is are distanced, so the interior world of intuition, creativity and imagination is freed. Once you become more adept and confident in your visualization you'll discover that your power of intuitive insight is released.

Right brain/left brain

Creative visualization works by releasing the constraining hold of the left brain – the logical, analytical side – and freeing the inspirational right brain. When we turn down the volume of the left brain in colour visualization, we give space for the song of the heart.

Our most inspired moments come when we are not consciously thinking about our concerns: instead, flashes of insight, strokes of genius and brilliant points of awareness are able to present themselves because our intellectual censor is not at work. That doesn't mean to say that the role of the left brain isn't vital, but to truly connect with your inner wisdom and creative essence you have to give your right brain a chance to breathe.

How Does Creative Visualization Improve Health?

Healing can come from within. There is overwhelming evidence that our mental state has a profound impact on our physical health. Amazing work carried out by the American cancer specialist Dr Bernie Siegel, shows how the power of positive thought can radically improve life-threatening conditions. Working hand in hand with traditional medicine, visualization can offer new dimensions for recovery.

Norman Cousins, author of *An Anatomy of Illness*, was diagnosed as having terminal cancer and given six months to live. He reflected on his life and felt that depression, anger and worry had contributed to his disease. If negativity was part of the reason he'd become ill, he concluded, then being positive and visualizing a new life might improve his chances of survival.

Norman searched for the most positive activity he knew and decided it was laughter. He rented comedy films, got friends to tell him jokes, send him humorous stories, and literally surrounded himself with fun and joy. He found that laughing for just five minutes relieved his chronic pain for hours, and visualizations strengthened his feeling of control over his illness. Now, many years later, he cites laughter and visualization, as well as the love of family and friends, as the main reasons for not only his survival but his continuing good health.

In illness, by using creative visualization, you can reduce feelings of anxiety, calm your breathing and, as a consequence, send messages of calmness throughout your cardiovascular system which in turn acts to reduce pain and distress. These mental processes influence your immune system and the hormones that circulate in your body and so actually change its physical structure. The boost to your immune system helps it to ward off those viruses that attack when you are feeling below par.

Creative visualization with colour is not successful in isolation: you need to think of yourself holistically to maintain optimum health. So you also need to think about your eating patterns and other aspects of your lifestyle. Visualization will enhance your own healing system – vital in view of our increasingly toxic environment.

How Do I know if Creative Visualization Can Help me?

Creative visualization is used by doctors, politicians, healers, neurolinguistic programmers, weightwatchers, competitors of all types, therapists, stress consultants, among others. It works with all sorts of people from all walks of life. The most important factor is whether you want to use it and whether you want it to work. If you want it to help you, then it will.

Ask yourself some questions: Are you totally content with every aspect of your life? Is your work fulfilling? Are your friendships warm and supportive or do friends seem to use you and put you down? What about your home? Do your surroundings reflect your personality or are they to other people's tastes? And what about the things that give you pleasure – hobbies, sport, daydreaming – do you spend time on them or do they get shoved to the bottom of the pile so you never seem to have time for yourself? If you do manage to snatch the odd half-hour do you feel self-indulgent and guilty?

If the answer to some of these is 'Yes,' then creative visualization will allow you to find the world you want rather than the one you have been conditioned to accept. You deserve the best, so now is the time to start making that a reality.

How Can I Use Creative Visualization in my Everyday Life?

You can use creative visualization to improve your physical attributes and mental, emotional and spiritual wellbeing – for instance, to enhance sporting performance, to lose weight, to increase successful problem solving, to improve health, to build confidence at work and in relationships, and to put you in touch with your own creative spark. It is a proven anti-stress technique and immune-system booster – crucial for anyone living in the fast lane where environmental pollution is the norm – and can combat disease.

When we think we will fail, we set in motion a train of thought that depresses our ability to think and act creatively and positively. We then stay in that comfortable, uncomfortable rut that we know so well. 'Oh, I've never been any good at interviews', says Helen and locks herself into a repetitive cycle of tired failure. She virtually wills herself to fail and fulfils her own prophecy. If she chooses, she can decide to succeed and set about harnessing the energy that comes from positive visualization, which operates on both the physical and mental level.

By visualizing positive outcomes instead of rehearsing catastrophic failures you give yourself a clear message that you can and will be successful. Creative visualization has been used to fight off illness, improve recovery rates after surgery, and to combat stress as well as increase self-confidence. The possibilities are vast; in fact, in many American and British hospitals visualization techniques are central to the therapeutic process and the results are truly stunning, as Jon Kabat-Zinn describes in his book *Full Catastrophe Living*. However, before we move on to the core of *Creative Visualization with Colour*, let us explore the impact of colour on our lives.

Colour Therapy

Look through a prism and you will see that everything in the world is surrounded by colour. From the beginning of time, people have recognized the healing power of colour. Our ancestors lived in the heart of natural colours, brightened their garments with vegetable dyes and ground pigments to paint on cave walls. Ancient civilizations invested colour with mystical power and honoured it as a manifestation of the light of their gods; rainbows, which revealed all the colours of the visible spectrum, were seen as heaven sent.

We all depend on light for our very existence, in fact we are beings of light. Without the life-giving force of the sun we would have no plants to give us food, no trees to take up toxic gases and produce oxygen, and without light and the reassuring glow of the moon and the stars we would know only the darkness of unending night. As we ultimately derive our health from the sun, so we bathe in the other glory of light that is colour, for colour is a form of light. Imagine, if you can, and it is not easy, a world completely devoid of colour. If that causes you an anxious shiver then you are already turned into the awesome power and meaning that pulses in the heartbeat of colour.

What is Colour for?

That may seem a silly question because colour just is. We are surrounded by it and usually we take if for granted, yet in the natural world of animals, plants and birds colour always has a purpose. It is there to attract, repel or conceal, to warn or communicate a whole range of messages. Think of the way some animals camouflage themselves so they have protection from their aggressors. Though we cannot physically change colour at will like a chameleon, we can change the colour of our clothes and make choices about the kind of impact we want to make.

Colour influences us because each colour affects the brain differently. When we see a colour the signal to our eyes is transmitted to a specific part of the brain according to the colour. Very bright, intense hues and shiny or glittery ones hit the most primitive, deep part of the brain, known as the 'limbic system'. This response is an emotional one and is probably connected to our biological heritage when we too used colour as direct communication. 'When I'm angry, I see red' reflects this link between physical reactions to colour and emotions. The brain regions involved in the system are mostly found in the left hemisphere, the home of intuition, creativity and inspiration, an area we'll be exploring further in later chapters.

It is interesting to note that visually impaired people are able to distinguish between colours. Theo Gimbel, in his *Colour Therapy Workbook*, describes how, probably as a compensatory factor, their sensitivity is enhanced so that they notice that the air over a red surface, for example, feels denser than the air next to blue. The different vibrations are sensed without seeing the different colours.

What is Colour Therapy?

Colour therapy involves the use of the energy vibrations of colour in diagnosis, and in healing and balancing the natural rhythms of the body. It encompasses a wide range of techniques and treatments. Colour therapists generally use the application of colour to restore balance within the body as a whole. It can also be applied to increase self-worth and to release blocks which cause illness and unhappiness. This book draws upon the immense healing potential of colour to povide a powerful additional dimension to creative visualization. Together they can be used to enhance relaxation, inspiration, protection, problem-solving and personal development.

Dr Edwin Brabitt interpreted the old wisdom of colour therapy in his book *The Principles of Colour Therapy*, published in 1878, which explained the intricacies of the energy systems which underpin its scientific foundation. He showed that every colour has a unique therapeutic value and that each one can be used to treat a particular physical or emotional problem. There are now many ways of working with colour, as you will discover later; suffice to say, Brabitt was one of the first to identify what each colour could do. For instance, he recognized that blue was a brilliant form of antiseptic; today, interestingly, more 'blue treatments' are used by colour therapists than any other colour.

Theo Gimbel, the founding father of colour therapy in Britain, provided more remarkable treatment results, not only on a physical level but on an emotional and spiritual level too. He found, for example, that blue light reduces blood pressure, eases the intensity of asthma attacks and aids relaxation. In contrast, red – at the opposite end of the spectrum – raises blood pressure and encourages over-activity, but helps with anaemia.

HOW DOES COLOUR THERAPY WORK?

Electromagnetic energy is invisible to the naked eye yet its power is unmistakable. The electromagnetic energy spectrum ranges from the longest energy waves (radio, television and radar), through shorter infrared rays to the shortest waves, the cosmic rays. You may have experienced the healing use of electromagnetic energy in x-rays and radium treatment; however, the visible rays – the eight colours of the spectrum – and their healing significance are something that we hear less about.

Scientific investigation has shown us that all matter is energy and energy is vibration. When we link these two concepts we find that each colour of the spectrum has its own vibrational frequency and that by directing colour vibrations we can maintain or change the vibrations of the body to a frequency which promotes health and harmony. When we absorb a colour vibration it travels via the nervous system and the chakras (energy centres) to the part of the body that needs it, and so maintains or restores our optimum state of wellbeing, or 'remembered wellness' as it is sometimes known. In effect, just as we tune in a radio to get the full signal strength and the best reception, we can use colour to obtain the best vibrational frequency for our unique needs, which fluctuate from day to day, hour to hour.

For a full exploration of these qualities, see the healing sections in the chapters on individual colours.

When giving a colour treatment, a therapist will usually choose one colour and its complementary. (The complementary colour is the one which appears opposite the given colour on the colour wheel, as you can see in the diagram on the inside front cover.) So, if someone was having a yellow treatment, as part of the process she would receive violet light to ensure the the chakras were balanced. And research by Theo Gimbel into high blood pressure showed that treatment with orange light relieved symptoms, but healing took place only when the complementary colour blue was included in the treatment programme.

How Old is Colour Therapy?

From the beginning of time, people have recognized the power of colour. Our ancestors lived in the heart of natural colours and dyed their garments with pigments gathered from earth and vegetation. Early societies invested colour with mystical significance. The Egyptians, for example, were passionate about colour symbolism. Their temples and amulets to ward off evil spirits dazzled with an intensity of hue, and temple priests wore chestplates of blue to symbolize the sacredness of their judgements. Colour meant something and could be 'read' by the society at large.

Ancient civilizations recognized colour as a manifestation of light and thus linked it to their gods. Gods were also associated with certain colours: Ceres, the Roman goddess of nature, is linked to the red poppy; Brahmanism is symbolized by the sacred colour yellow, which is also the colour worn by the Buddha; green is the sacred colour of Islam; and in Judaism the sacred colours are red, blue, purple and white. The early Greeks linked colour to universal harmony. Everywhere, colour was used therapeutically as well as creatively, and this included the use of gems and semi-precious stones.

In the Middle Ages colour was an essential part of heraldry. You may have come across heraldic coats of arms in historic buildings or in films about knights in battle. Special insignia which declared their status, family and history as a warrior were depicted on their armour or flags. These 'heralded' or announced their position in the world. In heraldic language white symbolized fate and purity, gold stood for honour, red meant courage and zeal, and blue expressed purity and sincerity. Black revealed grief and penitence, whilst green meant youth and fertility and orange showed strength and endurance. Princely purple was reserved for royalty and those of high birth.

The Power of Colour

Anyone involved in marketing ignores colour at their peril. Colour stirs our emotions and hits the brain faster than speech or the written word. We are influenced to buy when we see certain colours and our moods are swayed by the sales environment, which is why hospitals, shops, schools and public buildings employ consultants to select colours which drive home the corporate message. Let me give you an example of the negative effects of colour.

Albert Low, in his book *Feng Shui: The Way to Harmony*, tells the story of a red bridge which was the scene of many suicides. No one could understand why this particular bridge was so frequently chosen; to all intents and purposes it was just like all the other bridges in the area. Eventually, a group of local psychologists persuaded the council to paint it white and there were no further suicide attempts.

Exposure to red causes measurable reactions in our body: our blood pressure rises, our breathing and pulse rates increase and our brain waves become more highly stimulated. This colour has always been associated with heightened emotion, so someone in an intense state of anxious arousal and contemplating self-harm is more likely to be stimulated into action by the sight of a red bridge than a white one!

A whole range of therapeutic techniques use colour to promote wellbeing, from, at one end of the spectrum, everyday activities such as choosing certain colours for our clothes and homes, to the purist approaches used by Aura-Soma therapists. All approaches, though, are based on the fact that each colour has certain qualities which influence us, both positively and negatively. You may know this intuitively, which is why you spend a lot of time deciding what shade you want to paint your bedroom and what colour outfit you should wear for that all-important interview. Colour makes a difference; once you understand why this is so and how it works, you will increase your ability to consciously influence your personal life journey.

COLOUR ASSOCIATIONS

You will need a piece of paper or a notebook and something to write with. This practical exercise will introduce you to your own relationship to colour and creative visualization and give you a chance to experience the power of colour.

Close your eyes and think of the colour *red*. When you are ready – just a minute or so is enough – jot down any thoughts, feelings or images that come to mind. Whatever you note down is right, so let your ideas flow. Next, close your eyes and think of the colour *black*. Again, write down any thoughts, images or emotions that spring to mind.

Then look at your two sets of words. Is there a marked contrast? I asked three people to do this and this is what their combined lists included. For *red* they wrote: warm, fire, angry, heat, sunset, heart, blood, velvet, Valentine's Day, strength. In contrast, the *black* collection contained the words death, ebony, night, depression, coffee, crow, shadow and coal. Quite different moods were attached to the words and, of course, personal experiences influenced the choice. Look back at your list. What does it reveal about you?

At a very simple level this exercise confirms the fact that we attribute different qualities to different colours. There are a number of reasons why this happens; to explain we need to make a brief detour into the science behind the theory of colour visualization.

The Colourful Chakras: Tapping into your Energy Channels

Each energy centre or chakra (the Sanskrit word for wheel) is associated with a particular colour. Many different traditions throughout the world use these colour connections for health and healing. Yoga, for example, uses the energies of the chakras to enhance physical and mental health. Study of the chakras is based on the concept that there are major and minor points of energy in the body which affect our wellbeing. These points are used in acupuncture as well as other esoteric medical traditions.

The power of the chakras and their influence on our physical, emotional and spiritual wellbeing and development have been known for thousands of years, yet it is only in the recent past that the West has recognized their existence. Medical research into the endocrine systems in our bodies has shown how closely these relate to the chakras, confirming a wisdom that had been unacknowledged for centuries. We are finally accepting that just as the seas have currents and tides that explorers use to help in navigation, so we have internal energy streams that we can use to help us on our journey, be it physical, emotional or spiritual.

The chakras are the invisible sites of power in our bodies and each contains all the colours of the spectrum, though one colour is dominant in each case, as you can see in the diagram on the inside back cover. (You can explore these differences further in the chapters on individual colours.)

Ten energy channels run through the body, as Pauline Wills describes in her excellent *Reflexology and Colour Therapy Workbook*. They end at the soles of your feet and the palms of your hands. If for some reason these energy channels are blocked, then trouble is in store. The blockage is like a traffic jam: the energy gets snarled up, the flow is dammed and the resultant tension causes discord and dis-harmony and may provoke anger.

As you can see from the diagram, at the front of this book, seven major chakras are located in line with the spine. They are the Crown Chakra which is just above the top of the head, the Brow Chakra, the Throat Chakra, the Heart Chakra, the Solar Plexus Chakra, the Sacral Chakra and the Base Chakra. Each of these works with one of the endocrine glands in the physical body. The chakras and endocrine glands are interlinked; a traumatic experience, for instance, will affect a person's chakras so that the endocrine glands cannot work to their full potential and the flow of health-giving energy is restricted.

It may be easier to understand this invisible energy system if you think about other unseen mind–body links. For example, anxiety may not be apparent on the surface but it may affect us so deeply that we develop an ulcer. The latter is easily discovered by medical investigation, but the more subtle influences – the fear and worry – cannot be detected by the usual, visible means.

The Aura

The aura is a field of electromagnetic energy which surrounds each person. Like the chakras, an aura is not visible though some practitioners can see it or believe we can be trained to see it. The colours of the physical aura form a rainbow spectrum and are associated with specific vibratory wavelengths of the chakras. These waves hold the energy patterns which reveal the health of a person. When these are blocked then illness is likely to occur. The aura changes constantly according to our mood and state of health.

A Kaleidoscope of Colour Therapies

Colour is light made visible. In this overview of therapies that use colour, you will discover how its potential therapeutic energy is harnessed. Some of the therapies described need a qualified practitioner, others you can try alone.

Colour therapists recognize that when we are ill or unhappy our body gives out a distorted, disturbed pattern of vibrations. When the cells of any part of our body vibrate at the wrong frequency our organs are affected, and this in turn is manifested in illness. Colour therapists work to restore the delicate balance of the vibrational electro-magnetic components of the light which we see as colour. A therapist, after listening to the symptoms of the client, decides where there is an imbalance in the body and seeks to redress this. As our bodies are light sensitive, colour can be introduced to the site of the imbalance, by the use of stained glass, for instance. Light is transmitted through a specific colour glass in order to introduce balancing qualities back into the body. Using colour therapy we can thus rebalance any incorrect tuning and re-assert a balanced, beneficial frequency. There are many ways to do this.

Crystal and Gemstone Therapy

In the central dome of the healing temple in Atlantis, legend has it, the ceiling was made out of interlocking crystals and the daylight which shone through the quartz radiated all colours of the spectrum. The patterns of colour and the vibrations produced filled the temple, giving the ground-floor rooms which ringed the circumference specific colours and healing dimensions. The individual healing rooms resonated with light, and people who sought emotional, physical and spiritual treatment would be cared for in whichever 'colour' room was most beneficial.

Crystals, seemingly filled with coloured light, have always been held in reverence for their mystical qualities and their ability to intensify any light which passes through them. As well as being objects of beauty to be appreciated, crystals were also ground up and diluted or dipped in water, which was then drunk to cure disease. The energy of the quartz crystal, which is mainly used today instead of the prismatic diamond, is combined with colour to increase its potency. Light shone through coloured filters is then magnified or amplified by passing it through quartz crystal or particular gemstones, dramatically increasing their effect.

Crystals are still regularly used to bring back harmony and restore health. This is done by the use of a crystal light box containing a spectrum daylight bulb (never an ultraviolet one), a slotted area where different colours of stained glass can be inserted, and a quartz crystal which is placed on the stained glass. Hand-crafted stained glass makes the best colour filter as it provides the purest hues and has a density and vibration that artificial materials lack. After a consultation, the therapist directs the colour and crystal light to the physical spot or chakra which seems to be out of balance or blocked.

Sometimes polished gemstones are used instead of crystal, as some therapists feel their purity of colour and unadulterated, natural energy has more concentrated power to heal. In addition, chosen gemstones can be worn as pendants so that their vibrations can be absorbed by the wearer at all times.

Practitioners of Ayurvedic medicine have been using gemstones for thousands of years. They assert that crystals contain the energy and properties of the seven cosmic rays. Seven main gems are used. They are either burnt and the ash 'administered' to the patients, or soaked in alcohol so that the vibrations of the gem are taken up by the liquid, which is then drunk.

Aura-Soma

Aura-Soma is a non-intrusive, self-selected therapy which works by regenerating, revitalizing and rebalancing the human aura. The Aura-Soma system is designed to diagnose problems in the chakras then treat the client, who is offered a choice of four 'balance bottles' from a range of more than 90.

In this selection process, clients automatically choose the colours they need to bring them back into balance. To ensure that our energies flow in harmony – mind, body and spirit – each chakra must be fully open and in balance. The balance bottles comprise two separate colour mixtures relating to individual areas of the body according to their chakra links. The choice of colours holds the key to spiritual, mental, emotional and physical states and Aura-Soma. The therapy works as part of a holistic approach using counselling skills, colour awareness and healing.

Self-help Colour Therapy

We know that coloured light – that is, visible rays – influences animals and plants and so it is hardly surprising that human beings should also be subject to its power. What you need to know is how you can maximize its beneficial potential. Here are some suggestions.

What colour do you choose to surround yourself with at home? Is it plodding brown, safe and undemanding? Is it cool blue to dampen emotions? Or perhaps it is harmonizing green for balance. All colours can change your mood so you can induce wellbeing by picking those that you need for your personal living space. These colours will influence not only yourself but everyone who comes into your territory.

Using colour in your everyday life

This is a simple way to help yourself to health. Choose a colour from the colour wheel on the inside front cover. The energy vibration of the colour you are drawn to is what you need at this particular moment.

There are a number of things you can do next but first of all look up your chosen colour in the relevant chapter and read what its properties are. If you need the extra zest of orange, for example, wear something orange, rest against an orange cushion, or choose a piece of orange material to gaze on as you relax in a comfortable position. Drink in the colour until you feel you have absorbed its energy. When you have time, buy yourself a set of coloured cards from an art shop so that you can select a colour and focus on it whenever you feel lacking in energy.

The need for a particular colour vibration differs from day to day so you can use this technique whenever you need a boost. If one colour regularly appeals more than the others, you could introduce foods of this this colour into your diet to increase its effect.

Food

When you need an extra boost of energy or need to calm down, think about introducing specific food colour groups into your eating plan. For example, continuing with the orange theme, try carrots, peppers, sweet potatoes and, of course, oranges for additional warmth and vitality.

You will find a food section in each of the colour chapters.

Clothes

In the highly competitive environment of work, especially when moving into a new career, it is vital that we make that first impression count. Did you know that psychologists studying people's first impressions found that 93 per cent of the initial impact comes from appearance alone? Can you ignore the power of this statistic?

Because we live in a visual society and people are reading the signals you give off all the time, using colour effectively can be your key to success. Let it work for you, not against you. It is no secret that many major clothes retailers use image consultants to advise on how to offer balanced collections each season. Training programmes are run for fashion sales staff so they are able to advise customers more effectively on what suits them.

The 'Colour Me Beautiful' organization, pioneers in image consultancy, base their work on the theories of Johannes Itten, an artist working with the Bauhaus school in the 1920s in Germany. Itten devised a colour wheel which, as well as describing the colours and their complementaries, defined them in terms of whether they were 'warm' or 'cold'.

Yellow, yellow-orange, orange, red, and red-violet are warm, whereas, going the other way on the colour wheel, yellow-green, green, blue, blue-violet and violet are cold. After asking his students to choose their favourite colours, Itten realized that their choices complemented their skin tone, as well as their eye and hair colour. Today's image consultants use colour analysis to advise men and women on how to present themselves to optimize the impression they make. This in-depth process not only improves the visual impact a person can make, but also builds up confidence and self-esteem. Corporate customers abound and many newly appointed managers are introduced to the power of colour in personal presentation.

Plants

Monet was not only a stunning painter; he made his world famous garden at Giverny into a palette of impressionist colours. He may not have known that plants grown under different coloured lights have different growth patterns, as his countryman Ressier proved in 1783, but he knew the psychological impact of colour arrangement.

If you are a gardener you can plan colour to maximize both space and sensation. Monet created monochromatic borders using plants of the same colour but in different tones to create harmony. Elsewhere he used complementary colours next to each other to increase intensity, and cool colours such as blue, green and purple to create a receding effect. Warm colours such as red, yellow and orange do the opposite and seem to jump forward to catch our attention. Monet, like other truly creative gardeners such as Gertrude Jekyll, approached garden design as an artist makes a painting and used colour to dramatic effect.

Now you know about the dynamic impact colour can have in your life, it is time to explore how it links to a second equally powerful force, creative visualization. Here colour and creative visualization are combined in a focused way to give you the means to direct your life journey. Your vision and future can be your own creation.

Creative Visualization with Colour

The combination of creative visualization and colour allows you to intensify the ability of both to influence positive outcomes. When an athlete visualizes himself winning a race, for instance, if he includes the colour of the clothes he will be wearing on the day, if he sees himself tying his white racing shoes before the event and sees the finishing tape against his red top, he amalgamates the physical aspect of his experience with the creative visualization. Later, on the day of the race, as he ties those shoes and puts on his top, his mind and body will be already set up for success, without consciously thinking about it, as those visualized sensations flood back. The signals of the colours will reinforce his positive attitude, mentally and physically.

Once you know more about the vibrations of different colours and their properties, you can choose which to include in your visualization to amplify the power. If you have an infection, for example, as you visualize the inflamed area, send ripples of blue solution over it and feel it being soothed. The blue multiplies the healing aspect because its vibrational energy is linked with antiseptic qualities. Whether you want to lose weight, increase your ability to study or pass your driving test, include colour at the heart of the visualization because it is at the core of your being. By harnessing it in this way you will both honour it and reap wonderful rewards.

Colour Visualization and Stress

One of the greatest causes of disease at present, linked without doubt to the suppression of our immune systems, is destructive stress. I say destructive stress because not all stress is harmful; an increase in stress can galvanize us to make that extra effort, give us the burst of adrenaline that pushes us to peak performance. Unfortunately, relentless excessive stress at some point becomes counterproductive and damages our immune system.

If the effectiveness of our immune defence structure is undermined we suffer the consequences: greater susceptibility to disease, more likelihood of mental and emotional problems, decreased ability to concentrate, and all the rest. There is no doubt whatsoever that carrying high levels of stress over a long period can become life-threatening. It can lead to high blood pressure, strokes, heart disease and mental health problems. Cancer too has been linked to high levels of stress and many marriages collapse under the impact of acute or chronic stress. So, what has this to do with colour visualization?

When you feel stressed very often you can't stop and relax enough to take in your surroundings. Finding time to get yourself out of the house is hard enough, let alone sparing the time to stop and stare, to breathe in the wonders of nature – the trees in green bud, the glorious orange of the sunset or the magic in a bunch of snowdrops or a posy of pink roses. Because you don't make the time, you don't absorb their health-giving properties. You don't slow down enough – even for a minute or two – to let your body take a moment's rest to replenish your cells with energy.

The misery of negative thinking

Negative thinking has a physical impact. It suppresses the immune system, which is your own defence mechanism for warding off illness; it raises blood pressure and creates tension within your body. All this causes fatigue; you feel tired and worn-out no matter how much rest you get, and your physical strength gets worn down too. When this happens opportunistic infection can sneak in; the weaker your immune system, the easier it is for viruses to make the most of their opportunities and find a host to feed on.

Changing your view of life, becoming more positive and open to life-enhancing opportunities instead of those which encourage disease, can bring about change. You can put those viruses to sleep, set up a time of remission and learn to live your best life in a healthy way. Creative visualization with colour will enhance this process.

Colour Visualization with Plants

Plants provide stimulation for colour visualizations all year round. Whether you have a large garden, a window box or only space for house plants you can use plants for creative visualization. In addition, you can buy single flowers or bunches of flowers to aid the process.

Choose a plant which appeals to you and either put it in front of you about 3 feet away or sit out in the open near to the plant. Let your breathing find its own gentle rhythm and relax your muscles so that you feel in a quiet frame of mind.

Look very closely at the plant; notice its colours and textures. Then take your attention to one part, for instance the petals. Imagine that you are tracing their outline with your fingers. Feel this soft, velvety bloom. Let the aroma drift towards you, or imagine it if you are too far away. Focus on the colour for two minutes then close your eyes. Imagine the plant now in all its intricate details and try to re-create it in your mind.

Pause.

Let your mind create a garden full of your chosen plants. Feel yourself bathed in its colour, drenched in crystal light. Let the qualities of the colour surge through you. When you are ready, open your eyes and once again allow yourself to appreciate the natural beauty before you.

You can plant your garden in such a way that it gives you the colour changes you may need and want. Then, at any time, you can sit and contemplate the plants and your chosen colour. Let their vibrations reach you and breathe them into your heart. Let their colour flood your senses and stimulate your warmth, power and creativity.

Making Changes

Whatever it is that you wish to change, you can use creative visualization with colour as part of a positive process. Changes don't miraculously happen – well, not usually – but there are things you can do to make miracles more likely! First, you need to believe that change is possible; secondly, you must want to change; and thirdly, you have to put some effort into bringing about that change. Creative visualization using colour is a good way to start.

Using all your Senses

You need to be clear at the outset that visualization does not demand that you see what is happening. If I say 'imagine walking on a beautiful stretch of soft green moss', you do not have to 'see' the grass. If your favoured way to experience the world is not through your eyes, you may *feel* the moss, or *hear* the tread of a footfall, or *smell* the unique aroma of the moss, or *sense* it through your pores. Whichever way of experiencing the world you intuitively choose, you can still reap the rewards of visualization. Use whichever way suits you.

Enhance your Visualizations with Crystals

As we saw earlier, crystals and gemstones have powerful properties which can enhance work with colour. Before starting a creative visualization with colour, choose a crystal from the appropriate colour range and sit with it in your hand for two or three minutes to absorb the energy it gives off. Alternatively, place it in front of you, let your eyes focus on it softly and let the vibrations come to you. Using crystals in this way is an excellent preparation for any visualization.

In the chapters on individual colours you will find a section listing stones within that colour range. Read about their particular properties, choose one which feels right for you – trust your intuition, you will pick the one you need – then concentrate on it.

Preparation

In creative visualization, it is very important that you feel relaxed and at ease on your guided journey. If possible find a room or a space in your home where you will not be disturbed and where you can, for a limited period of time, be free from all interruptions. You will know when is the best time for you and how you want that space to be organized.

Some people find quiet music in the background helps them to relax and creates the kind of atmosphere that is conducive to inner awareness. You may find that a lighted candle will also enable you to travel more easily. The aim is to find a way of making yourself as comfortable as possible in preparation for a journey into the deep treasure domains of your unconscious.

In order to follow the visualizations, take the instructions that follow at a gentle pace so that you have time to explore the images at suitable points. It is a useful idea to have someone else read the words to you or to record them and play your tape once you are relaxed and settled. By doing this you will find it easier to concentrate, because having to refer to the written words can disturb the flow.

Relaxation routine

The relaxation process is a central part of creative visualization with colour, and if you go through this process before each visualization you will reap the greatest benefits.

You are in control

The colour visualizations in this book are unlikely to cause any distress or discomfort; however, if at any time you do not like the way your journey is going or you are unhappy with anything that is happening, you can change it. You can do this by taking your attention to a place that you have enjoyed in the past. You can simply stop the direction that the visualization is going in and go somewhere else. At all times you are fully in control.

Affirmations

At the end of each visualization you will find some affirmations; repeat these to yourself to strengthen your positive experiences.

Find yourself a comfortable place in your quiet room. Take your shoes off. Either lie or sit down. It really does not matter whether you are lying or sitting as long as your spine is straight. If you are sitting make sure your feet are flat on the ground. This is to keep you grounded and in contact with the earth at all times. If you are lying on your back, the ground will of course be in contact with the whole length of your body.

Once you are resting comfortably, close your eyes and be aware of your body either lying on the floor or sitting on the chair. Be aware of the weight of your body and how it meets the supporting surface. Be aware of your breathing and know that you are in a safe, supportive space.

Take your attention down to your feet first of all, and scrunch your toes as tight as you can, then relax them. Be aware of the tension when you tighten your toes and notice how you feel when you let go of that tension.

Now let your attention travel to your calves and tighten the muscles at the back of your legs and then release. Feel the hardness as you tense your muscles and the softness when you let go.

Allow your attention now to go to your thighs. Tighten those thigh muscles and feel the tension as you do so, then let go.

By now you have felt the tension throughout your legs. As you relax, imagine that whatever tension is left is dissolving out through the chair or the floor. It is melting away, through to the ground below where it can disappear into the vastness of the earth.

Now let your awareness go to your stomach. Tighten the muscles there and really feel them holding in, clamping down. Next let those muscles fully relax, allowing them to be free to rest, with no holding in on your part. We often hold anxiety in the stomach area so it is truly liberating to allow whatever fears and worries you have to just soften and melt away, as the mist does in the early morning when the sun warms the earth. Like the mist, your fears will disappear to reveal a warm security.

Take your attention now to your chest area, the area which encloses and protects your heart. Tense your chest muscles and then relax. Feel your whole chest area expand and then settle, taking all the space it needs to let your heart and lungs work smoothly. Let any rigidity yield to open acceptance.

Now take your attention to your fingers and make a tight fist. Really tighten those fingers so that your knuckles turn white, and then relax them. Stretch your fingers and let all the tension from your arms drip from your fingertips down into the earth to be absorbed and changed into positive energy.

Next take your attention to the area around your neck and shoulders. Tense them up and feel them tighten; feel the energy that it is lodged there, energy that can so often cause stiff necks and shoulder strain. Allow all that pressure to ease away, to soften, leaving you free of tension.

Finally, screw up the area around your eyes. Really feel the tension. Hold that grimace, and then relax. Imagine the lines that you made when you were so tense simply softening away to leave you smooth and stress free.

By now the relaxation part is almost over. You are just about ready to begin your journey. But before you embark, let your inner eye rove through your body looking for any remaining points of tension. If you find a knotted area, simply make that part even tenser then relax. You may need to shift your position a little to become more comfortable. Do this now so that you are ready for your journey.

Summary

Use visualization to help you reach your goals and to intensify the powerful imagery, then combine it with colour to affirm your vision. For instance, if you are studying for an exam, visualize yourself in a calm state reading the set paper in the examination room. See yourself in your favourite, confidence-boosting clothes that you will wear for the exam. See yourself smiling as you recognize that the questions are ones for which you have prepared. Be aware of feelings of quiet pleasure as you write your successful answers.

Creative visualization with the added dimension of colour will help you depart from the shores of old, safe, worn-out comfort zones that trap you in familiar ruts. You will find various exercises and a variety of techniques to set you thinking in new ways that go beyond those comfort zones so you can pursue your dreams and arrive at the new horizons waiting at the edge of the map. It's time to sail in the luminous sea of promise; you will find the departure point in Chapter 2, 'Red: Warming the Heart'.

2

Red: Warming the Heart

If I see one dilemma with the Western man, it's that he can't accept how beautiful he is. He can't accept that he is pure light, that he's pure love, that he's pure consciousness, that he's divine.

BABA RAM DASS

As the first colour of the rainbow, red takes its primal position. It is the colour of love, blood and the essence of life. Red and orange are in the molten lava thrown out by unpredictable volcanoes, the burning fires of passion and the heat of the moment. Red symbolizes the very life force that keeps our physical world alive and throbbing.

Passionate, Powerful Red

Red is nature's sexual signal. The pulsing energy of blood surging through our veins indicates emotions that can take us to ultimate exaltation or sorrow, creativity or destruction. When passion floods the body our skin reddens or flushes with warmth and excitement and our lips become redder, which is why red lipstick was always associated with 'scarlet' women. We imitate this state of sexual arousal without even being aware of it. How?

Our cosmetics industry knows how! Skin colour has always been regarded as a vital element in beauty. The enhancement of natural colour plays an important part in heightening sexual attraction. Its origins can be traced back to ancient Egypt where red dyes were used to emphasize racial pride and distinction.

Red, the most emotionally compelling colour, at the 'hot' red end of the spectrum, denotes ardent love, valour and energy. It governs the gonads, the reproductive organs, the ovaries and the testes and all aspects of sexuality. Mars, the planet and the god of war, are linked to this colour, as is the mother goddess of India. She is always represented in red because she is associated with the principle of creation. Buddhists call red the colour of activity and creativity.

Intense physical activity makes us 'red in the face', as our skin is suffused with blood, which is another reason why red is associated with sexual activity. There are many other sexual connections: 'painting the town red', sexy red underwear, the red of the blood that comes when virginity is taken or lost, and 'red light' districts (from the time when prostitutes advertised their premises by hanging a red lamp in their windows).

This vital crimson energy is reflected in the names of passionate, larger-than-life characters: Scarlett O'Hara, the passionate heroine in *Gone With The Wind*; Red Adair, the man who puts out oil slicks which have caught fire or tames oil rigs burning out of control. Red robes were worn in ancient Rome to symbolize sacrifice and love, and red was a colour Cleopatra no doubt wore to maximize her impact.

Blood red

The symbol of spilt blood has always been associated with sacrifice of some sort, from the biblical sacrificial lamb to the revenge killings in *Romeo and Juliet*. In Sanskrit, *ruh-ira* means both red and 'blood', and when we 'see red' blood might be drawn. There is an Arabic proverb 'Blood has flowed, danger is past', indicating that such blood sacrifices end feuds. Although this is not always the case, as we know from sectarian murders as far apart as Ireland and the Middle East, it shows how such primitive drives still lurk below our mask of civilization.

A Roman general when he returned home in triumph after battle would be carried in a chariot pulled by four white horses dressed in gilt armour which symbolized the glory of the sun. In addition the general's face would be painted red, emphasizing both his fighting power and his creative energy.

Red is courageous and, in extremes, over-confident. In heraldry, red is known as 'gules', the sign of bravery and zeal. The knights who wore red were expected to fight valiantly, until death if need be. Again and again red is associated with blood lust and power. Even earlier than the Knights Crusaders, the ancient Greeks wore scarlet when they recited the *Iliad*, to symbolize the bloody battles recorded in the poem.

Destructive, dangerous red

Because red can go to extremes and get rowdy, it is also associated with mischief and mayhem. It has the power to bring about destruction. Red-hot lava can engulf cities – Pompeii, for example, when Mount Etna erupted. Negatively, red typifies cruelty, anger and sin, and the warmonger or aggressive bully.

Domineering extremism is another downside of red. The 'red rag to a bull' syndrome symbolizes the colour's provocative nature. It can make a difficult situation worse and put you in a hot spot.

A Rush of Red

A short exposure to red, even though it has the slowest wave length of all the colours, speeds things up, gives you that vibration to quicken the pulse that prompts activity. Red encourages you if you are timid; it gets you noticed so you don't have to make the first move yourself. People will come to you instead of you having to go to them. Red has the push to drive you on. It's a stimulator.

It also has a 'shout' quality which is extremely useful as an attention-grabber. Red warning lights stop us in our tracks, wires that carry heavy voltage are often sheathed in red, and computer designers who want to emphasize particular functions use red interface information to ensure that users respond to the data given. Red is a 'touch me' colour so is often used on buttons and knobs, inviting action where alertness is needed. Warm colours, including red and orange, are very useful in situations where safety is of paramount importance.

Interior designers favour reds in restaurant décor because, as well as inducing a feeling of wellbeing, they influence clients to 'eat and go' rather than linger. Time appears to pass more slowly in red surroundings and diners feel they've been there longer than they actually have. Also, as red is said to increase the appetite, they will probably feel hungrier and order more food – and thus spend more money. However, in more exclusive restaurants where owners want clients to be pleasurably excited but not rushed, they may choose the colour burgundy – more subtle and elegant.

The next time you are too busy to cook and buy fast foods from your local supermarket, check the packaging. What colours do you notice? The majority of fast foods are contained in red wrappings because of the colour's connection with speed.

Mythical Connections

The life-giving quality of red has been recognized by diverse cultures through history. The Tjet, a red stone, was placed with the dead body of an Egyptian Pharaoh so the newly deceased could symbolically take the blood of Isis to fuel his life beyond earth. The Ab, or heart amulet, preserved the soul that was in the physical body.

Earlier, in prehistoric times, the dead were buried in red ochre, or in some instances their bones were painted red, because it was thought that red blood marked the boundary between life and death. Painting bones may have been seen as a way of giving renewed life in the world beyond.

Chakra Connection

location→ The Base Chakra is at the end of the coccyx, where the spine ends. This chakra is called the Muladhara, from the Sanskrit word for 'root', and its colour is red. In Eastern teaching it is symbolized by a deep-red lotus flower with four petals. Situated as it is, this chakra radiates downwards, connecting us to the earth and physical survival. This connection is symbolized in an ancient tradition in which blood was poured into the ground to ensure fecundity and increase fertility.

The Base Chakra contains our primal energy, the Kundalini Shakti. It is the centre of our physical energy and vitality and our sense of will and power. It is also associated with the gonads and thus sexuality. If this chakra is blocked a person will have low energy levels and little enthusiasm for everyday tasks and life in general, plus a lowered sex drive. blocked→

Healing with Red

Red is the symbol of life and strength. This vital colour splits the ferric salt crystals into iron and salt. The red corpuscles absorb the iron and the salt is eliminated by the kidneys and the skin. This makes it a good colour treatment for anaemia or iron deficiency. As red can be so stimulating its properties are not used a great deal in therapies for anxiety or emotional disturbances.

Faber Birren, an American colour analyst, reported to the International Colour Association's 2nd Congress on the effect red has on the human body:

> **Exposure to red can increase body temperature because of increased heart action. Warmth of it tends to raise blood pressure, respiration rate, brain activity and to prod the automatic nervous system. Dimness and coolness of colour tend to have reverse effects.**

Probably because of its connection with bright, healthy blood, red has always had a place in healing practices. As a very powerful energizer and stimulant it increases energy, raises body temperature, enhances the appetite and improves circulation. In ancient China, a ruby was worn to promote long life and a red ribbon was tied to a child's pigtail to harness healing energy. Red ribbons and scarves were also used as cures. 'Tie a red ribbon around the neck to cure a nosebleed' is an old adage in certain parts of the UK. In each of these examples you can see how the warmth and vitality of the red vibration is used to counteract problems induced by cold or where the blood circulation has gone awry, as in the case of nosebleeds.

HEALING CRYSTALS AND GEMSTONES

- **Agate** – calms the body, mind and spirit; good for healing in general.
- **Bloodstone** – keeps the chakras balanced and builds self-confidence; improves liver function and psychosomatic pain; attracts creativity.
- **Carnelian** – helpful for fertility, impotence, menstruation.
- **Garnet** – a dream inducer; helpful in matters of love and as a general tonic.
- **Jasper** – useful for urinary problems and blood disease.
- **Kundite** – a pink stone for emotional support; opens the heart to trust, especially after fear brought on by others.
- **Obsidian** – good for countering negative moods.
- **Rose quartz** – good for building self-esteem, emotional balance and friendships, including self-love.
- **Ruby** – beneficial for emotional and spiritual problems; good for when you are feeling run down; helps you feel uplifted and energized; builds self-confidence.

Healthy Colour Eating

Red peppers and tomatoes are good for fighting off damage from free radicals, those tiny particles that can severely damage our DNA structure and trigger off diseases such as cancer. Tomatoes are fast becoming the star in this health arena, particularly cooked ones. Research shows they contain lycopene, a very powerful antioxidant which might in particular reduce a man's risk of prostate cancer as well as being helpful for both sexes in a more general way.

Carrots are high in betacarotene and other antioxidants which strengthen our immune system. So this is another good orange colour to include in your diet. Eat them raw rather than cooked.

Lilian Verner-Bonds and Joseph Corvo, whose work is covered in their book *The Healing Power of Colour Zone Therapy*, explain that red acts as a strong detoxifier because it helps to get rid of waste products and remove negativity from your mind, body and spirit. They also point out red's value as a general tonic, especially if you have been feeling low and depressed.

Making Changes with Red

Nothing in life is fixed, change is always right next to us.

The morning star is like a man;
he is painted red all over;
that is the colour of life.

Traditional Pawnee chant

The Pawnee chiefs offered this traditional invocation, calling on the power of red to enrich their lives and give strength to their hunting, planting and reproduction.

Use the energy of red to bring about positive change in your life.

Creative Visualization with Red

The butterfly

Before doing this visualization, make sure you are relaxed by following the routine on pages 23–5 in Chapter 1.

 record

Once your breathing has become calm and steady, with your next breath imagine you are lying on a red velvet couch. It is soft and luxuriant. You feel a gentle heat rising up into your back. Notice the glow of vital energy being carried by your blood to circulate all around your body. Be aware of this warmth that fuels your ability to be independent, to be your own person when you choose to be.

As you lie in the red aura that now surrounds you, allow the fertility that is your essence to become more accessible. Feel this rising from the Base Chakra at the base of your spine, as a glowing light reaching through your body right up to your eyes. Feel your body filling with this orange-red glow and warmth.

Pause.

Each time you breathe in, feel the energy strengthening your flowering creativity. Breathe out previous doubts and uncertainties. You are and always have been a person of vision and now you can release the positive ideas that have been hidden. Feel your pulsing creativity surface, bringing forth new ideas. Perhaps they are solutions to problems. Perhaps these thoughts show you how you can alter situations, change problematic relationships. Whatever the issues, red gives you both the power and the energy to change.

Pause.

As you settle in your sphere of red, you begin to see in front of you a timeless point of transition. As you watch it becomes clearer and you see a small elongated shape. It is a dark-red chrysalis which holds a butterfly in waiting.

Pause.

Now you see minute movements. Notice the shiny cover which offers protection to the inner life. With your next in-breath remember times in your life when you felt small and were on the point of change. In this present safe space, recall your feelings as you watch nature's miracle of transformation in front of you.

Before your gaze, you see the top of the chrysalis crack, just a small opening at first but it then grows bigger and bigger until finally the tiny head of a butterfly begins to emerge. Take time to witness the birth of this gossamer creature. Notice how it works so hard to make its way into the blue sky that awaits. See the struggle as it finally frees itself from its outgrown shelter.

Pause.

See how the butterfly rests until its wings are filled with life energy ready for flight. See the beauty in its shape, colour and design. As you watch the delicate fluttering of its wings, you notice a shaft of orange light coming through your red sphere. This orange beam gently energizes the butterfly before it tentatively tries its wings.

Pause.

Be aware of your breathing, of the warmth in your heart as you too realize you can make transitions if you choose. This butterfly symbolizes your potential to renew yourself.

Completely assured now, the exquisite butterfly rises in the orange ray, upwards and upwards into the blue infinity that lies beyond. Your heart fills with love for the beautiful transition you have witnessed and you are strengthened, knowing that the love in the universe surrounds you just as the cocoon protected the emerging chrysalis. Gradually you notice that your red sphere is drifting away, to be replaced by a protective white brilliance. Feel your body in the space in which you are sitting or lying, and return to your place of comfort and safety.

When you are ready, open your eyes and stretch your wings.

Affirmations

- **I am open to loving kindness.**
- **I am free to grow, to change and to love.**
- **I give myself the gift of forgiveness.**
- **I am open to new ideas, new friends and new awareness in my life.**

Time to reflect

This visualization may have helped you to recognize areas of your life that are in need of renewal. Maybe you saw a new you trying to emerge in the same way as the butterfly. It might be a struggle but it will be well worth it if you gain the freedom to soar to unexplored heights once you have accepted your potential.

Make some notes about what you would like to change. This will help you when you come to the final chapter 'Sifting for Gold' .

Creative Planting

Red and orange will bring warmth and drama into your garden or home. There is a vast range of plants to choose from – and not only flowers; many trees and shrubs have bark, stems, berries or leaves in fiery colours. For a softer effect go for more delicate shades of pink.

PLANTING SUGGESTIONS – RED, ORANGE AND PINK

Spring	Marmalade bush, Brazilian firecracker, *Cornus alba* (red-barked dogwood), *Beluta ermanii* (a birch with dusty-pink bark), Easter cactus.
Summer	Red roses, *Potentilla* 'Red Ace', fuchsias, busy lizzies, pelargoniums, *Nicotiana* 'Crimson Rock', lantern tree.
Autumn	Red chrysanthemums, pink asters, red-hot pokers, *Gerbera jamesonii*, *Acer palmatum*, Virginia creeper.
Winter	Holly and rowan (for their red berries), poinsettias, winter cherry.

Personal Preferences

We all have certain colours that particularly appeal to us. These two pieces reflect the variety of emotions evoked by the colour red.

WARM RED BLANKET

Red makes me think of bright-red blood, then I remember the red of the post boxes in Britain. Sunshine, positive determination, energy, brightness like a gorgeous blanket covering the ground. It's very warm and bright and welcoming. I feel warm and pleasant inside, wrapped in my snugly red blanket; no one can touch me or come near me. No one else is around, my blanket is covering the world. I don't move, just sit and cuddle. It is warm and beautiful – no bad thoughts or feelings about myself or who I am, what I have to deal with and put up with. I am cocooned away from everything. There is no other colour in the world. Just red.

Trish

VIGOROUS RED

I associate red with vigour, liveliness. It is outgoing, full of enthusiasm and is bright and appealing. It's also the colour of my favourite football team, Manchester United, who I have followed since I was a boy. I am a regular fan of Salford Reds too. It's my favourite rugby team and I have always supported them. Hence red is associated with things dear to me. I've owned several red cars, and still own one.

Frank

VARIATIONS ON A THEME

Orange

Orange is the next colour in the spectrum after red, but its energy is a quieter, more restrained and sustaining energy, as you will see. Made up of two colours, red and yellow, the colour orange is a good mixer, a sociable colour that creates opportunity. It has the warmth, enthusiasm and energy of red, combined with the knowledge and creativity of yellow. Some call orange 'the seal of the soul'.

Chakra Connection

Orange is the colour assigned to the Sacral Chakra, which is between the navel and the top of the pubic bone. It is symbolized by an orange lotus with six petals which radiates the colour orange. This energy centre is ruled by the moon, which is associated with water and affects the movement of fluids in the body, as well as the more refined aspects of love and wisdom.

The abdomen and kidneys, the gut and the intestines are all associated with orange and all deal with the way we digest our food. Orange is used as a healing colour for food assimilation problems, anorexia, and for intestinal or bowel disorders. Orange is physical intuition – our 'gut feelings', an inner awareness that comes unexpectedly to our aid, which we can choose to respond to or not.

The adrenal glands are just above the kidneys and are the 'fight or flight' controllers governing this chakra. The adrenaline rush we feel when we are in danger, or in an emergency, is caused by the adrenal glands pumping out survival juices.

Healing with Orange

Orange enables us to create a balance between our mind and body. In colour therapy it can be used for the treatment of kidney stones and gall bladder problems – and is helpful in cases of muscle spasm and cramp. Orange increases immunity and helps in all digestive ailments. In addition, orange is said to be good in cases of shock, bereavement, trauma, rape or divorce.

Depression responds well to the stimulation of orange, perhaps because it reaches through to the deepest layer of our psyche, to the primeval warmth of the life-giving sun. Also, it reminds us of harvest time and the orange fruits of the earth, symbols of reward after toil. It enhances feelings of joy and happiness which is why, for some people, orange increases sexual potency.

HEALING CRYSTALS AND GEMSTONES

- **Amber** – a highly calming stone, good for balancing energies; used by healers as protection against taking on others' pain; helps with earache and urinary and nervous system problems.
- **Hematite** – relieves stress, particularly during air travel; improves energy levels and heart function.
- **Orange calcite** – improves awareness and self-confidence; increases vitality.

- **Tiger's eye** – increases confidence, will power and insight; reduces hypochondria.
- **Topaz** – improves blood circulation and helps calm the body; good for intellect and brings good luck; said to aid psychic development.

Creative Visualization with Orange

'Fire light, star bright'

Go through the relaxation exercise on pages 23–5 as a preparation for this visualization.

Imagine you are standing in an open space, a clearing in a wood or on a beach, before a brightly burning fire. The dark starry night wraps you in its great mystery. As you look into the glowing orange and red depths of the fire, be aware of the warmth that it radiates to your body. Feel suffused with the vibrant energy.

With your next in-breath notice how the fire becomes bigger, throwing flames higher and sending diamond sparks up to the stars. It is not a fire that can burn you; instead, it is the fire of creative problem-solving and achievement which energizes you. The smell of woodsmoke wafts through the air and you feel at one with nature and all the generations before who have looked into the heart of orange fire and known comfort.

As you look deeper and deeper into the centre you begin to sense a creative intelligence in the fire. You feel an awareness of your own coolness, but notice that the fire recognizes your sense of isolation which can keep you from your deepest warmth. The fire has the power to burn away any self-defeating habits and so release your positive potential.

Bring to mind one area of your life which needs to be cleansed, purified, released or revitalized. It could be a habit you want to change, a relationship which has dulled, a problem with a friend or colleague, or perhaps a physical challenge which is causing some distress. When you have found the issue you wish to focus on, hold it in your mind.

Pause.

Ask yourself what it is that needs to be changed. What outcome would make you feel happier?

Pause.

Be aware of any pictures, scenes or symbols that appear in the fire. These will help you to understand the next steps on the path to total wellbeing.

Pause.

In the brilliant warmth from the orange flames and yellow and red embers, gaze into the fire once more and know that any worn-out attitudes and habits you need to discard can be thrown into this fire. See the fire devour them. As you watch you sense a purification ritual is taking place. In future your dreams and visualizations will communicate your own inner wisdom to help you find new ways to live more fully in mind, body and spirit.

Pause.

Gently take your attention away from the fire and back to the comfort of the room, taking with you a feeling of rekindled awareness of your own ability to resolve difficulties and lead the kind of life you want to lead.

Affirmations

- **My creativity glows even in the darkest hours.**
- **I am filled with the radiant warmth of the universe.**
- **I discard the outworn past and live in the wonderful possibilities of now.**

Personal Preferences

ORANGE BLOOMS

Immediately I think about the colour orange I see sunsets over deserts, red and yellow blending into a darkening landscape. The night draws in and orange is the lamp that puts the sun to bed. Orange is the changer, cooling the energy of the glaring white sun of an Eastern sky, or a Middle Eastern terrain where mirages rise from the hot sand. Skies dramatic blue, and later a reduced intensity, heat subsiding.

I remember beautiful orange blooms in the Australian desert, highlighted against the dark red-orange earth of the outback. It is a colour that seeps through me from the setting sun to the rich earth, giving new energy and hope.

Lola

ORANGE AND GOLD

Whenever I think of orange, it always comes tinged with gold and I think of Scotland when the leaves on the trees are changing. I think of driving up the motorway then off onto the smaller roads, getting further and further away from the busy city where I live. Finding forests where all the scenery has different shades of orange, gold and yellow, and then walking through the trees. Through a clearing is a stream, and then I can sit and do nothing but listen to the quiet.

Kate

Pink

Pink is red with the addition of white, which softens the intensity of powerful red. It's a blush and a world seen through rose-tinted spectacles. When pink is positive it is feminine, gentle, accessible; it neutralizes aggressiveness. Some prison cells are painted pink to calm violent inmates. Gentle rose pink represents sweet love, the quietened passion of red, but it sometimes has a twist which makes it not so innocent!

Shocking-pink lipstick invites a more provocative response than the innocent candyfloss-coloured party dresses of little girls. Schiaparelli, the Parisian fashion guru who introduced Shocking Pink, defied the usual notions of pink and turned it into a colour screaming for attention. Another dazzling pink is fuchsia. Try either if you want to be noticed.

When you are 'in the pink' you have an abundance of flowing, natural energy, but in its negative guise, pink is seen as weak, pathetic, unimportant, dependent and lacking in confidence. This stems from its connection with baby girls, symbolizing a soft, undeveloped and naive quality.

SHIMMERING PINK

I always feel that pink is the colour of friendship. It is so comforting, from soft, baby pinks to the shades of seashells, Blackpool rock and candyfloss which make me think of the seaside holidays of my childhood. There are so many associations with pink, such as piglets, fluffy angora sweaters and the fluorescent, luminous, shimmering-pink lipstick I used to wear with a shocking-pink Lycra dress. Now, though, I like the cool sophistication of coral, but I still think of pink as a friend who has been with me all through my life. And when I get old I'm going to get a pair of shocking-pink slippers with ribbons on!

Barbara

Now it is time to travel to the cooler world of blue.

3

Feeling Blue

Blue, darkly, deeply, beautifully blue.

ROBERT SOUTHEY

If you think about the colour blue, what first crosses your mind? Is it the vast expanses of the sky, the endless sea, or perhaps the intense blue of sparkling sapphires. Almost without exception, when people visualize blue there is a sense of spaciousness, eternity and spirituality. This is not necessarily a religious sense of spirit; sometimes it can mean feeling at one with nature or feeling part of the universe in which the earth spins.

When you next stand beneath a cloudless summer sky, let your gaze rise to the majesty, peace and infinity of the blue. Allow yourself to feel the connection with all those who have looked up at the sky and felt awe. Think of all those who clothed themselves in sky-blue and brought a little bit of heaven into their dress to remind them of that which goes beyond everyday worries.

Blue: Bearer of Truth

Blue signifies wisdom, divine eternity and human immortality. Blue is the colour of the clear sky that equates with clear thinking. The Egyptians used blue to represent truth and, as if confirming this view, generations later blue became the colour of the Aquarian age and Aquarians are called 'seekers of truth'.

Whilst white symbolizes absolute truth, the blinding truth that you cannot avoid, sky-blue signifies a truth that is revealed and understood in a more gentle way. The negative side of blue represents an aloof, detached quality.

The Spiritual Connection

As American researcher Faber Birren noted in his book *The Symbolism of Colour*: 'The body of man is red, his mind is yellow and his spirit is blue.'

Blue symbolizes a less ardent love than red – a cooler, more spiritual relationship. It is not linked to expressions of wild physical passion but to a more thoughtful, cerebral profession of love.

For the ancient Greeks, blue was associated with Zeus and Hera, the gods of heaven, and Aphrodite, the goddess of love. Some say that blue is darkness made visible and is an attribute of Jupiter and Juno, god and goddess of heaven. It is the colour of the Archangel Michael, and the bodies of the Hindu gods Krishna and Vishnu are always depicted in an intense, vibrant blue to highlight their divinity.

> **Blue colour is everlastingly appointed by the Deity to be a source of delight.**
>
> John Ruskin

Royal blue is the colour of King David, the most important leader of the Jewish people. This shade is also the colour of Nuit, the Egyptian goddess of night who symbolized wisdom.

Blue is the colour of protection, the calm and peace which encourages inspiration, devotion, peace and tranquillity. Mary, mother of Jesus, also known as the Queen of Heaven and Madonna, is usually painted wearing blue robes. And like Kwan Yin, the Far Eastern goddess of mercy, Mary symbolizes protection, compassion and faithfulness. Peace, security and spiritual wisdom are their attributes.

The similarities between Mary, Aphrodite, Hera and Kwan Yin are easy to spot: their robes symbolize their heavenly connection as well as eternal devotion, and they each symbolize spiritual wisdom, faith and integrity.

Blue is also the colour of femininity and the new moon.

My Blue Haven

> **One night I walked beside the sea on the deserted beach. The deep blue sky was streaked with clouds of a deeper blue than the primary blue of an intense cobalt, and others of lighter blue, like the bluish whiteness of the Milky Way. Against the blue background the stars shone brightly, greenish, yellow, white and very**

pale pink, sparkling more like precious stones . . . opals, emeralds, lapis lazuli, rubies, sapphires.

Vincent Van Gogh

Blue is the safe haven which we all need, and throughout time people have unconsciously acknowledged the connection between sky-blue and heaven. Native Americans saw blue as the colour of heaven and peace.

The nave of a church is so named because symbolically the church is a ship that carries people on their spiritual journey through life. Often this central part of the building is painted in the purity of light blue, colour of the heavenly spheres and place of sanctuary. And throughout history heraldic coats of arms have used blue and 'azure' to symbolize piety and sincerity.

Mythical Connections

Blue is the colour of Celtic bards and poets, and the priests of ancient Egypt wore blue breastplates to mark the sacredness of their judgements.

To prevent being cursed by the evil eye, our earliest ancestors would war round blue discs painted with an eye, or a necklace with a piece of turquoise. The idea was that the evil eye would be attracted to the bright colour and not look into the eyes of the person wearing the amulet, and so would not snatch away their soul.

Today Tuareg tribesmen continue to paint themselves in dramatic blue dyes as they have done from time immemorial. They believe it strengthens them against adversaries and protects them. This custom was held by the Druids too, once again showing how interconnected we all are, no matter how far apart we live.

Chakra Connection

The Throat Chakra, symbolized by a blue lotus with 16 petals, acts as a channel between the heart and the mind. When energy is blocked here, there can be problems such as laryngitis, sore throats, loss of voice and the inability to speak up.

The voice is a channel of energy. It can tell us so much about the speaker. We can, for instance, detect the warm voice of someone who speaks from the heart, the sexy tones of someone whose energy comes from the Sacral Chakra, or the detached coolness of someone who speaks from the intellect.

Think about your own voice and what you express or conceal. Do you get a lump in the throat because you bite back tears? Do you get a stiff neck when you repress anger? Do you lose your voice when you no longer want to communicate? The Throat Chakra tells you a lot about self-expression, so take a few minutes to reflect on your communication style.

Healing with Blue

> **Nature is so beautiful and clean, the ice sparkling white with blue shadows on fresh fallen snow, set against the growing daylight and the glittering blue sky.**
>
> Fridtjof Nansen, Antarctic explorer

Colour is reflected light, as we saw in Chapter 1. The blue part of the light spectrum vibrates at a slower rate than red, for example, and so gives off a cooler energy. The famous Arab physician, Avicenna, who created a colour diagnosis and treatment chart, found that red acted as a stimulant whilst blue cooled the body. In 1958 Robert Gerard proved this when he discovered that red light raised blood pressure, whilst blue light lowered it.

Blue is a good antidote to stress because it slows things down, including the activity of over-stimulated brain waves. Hospital walls are often painted blue because the colour is thought to have a calming effect on patients who are over-anxious or hyperactive. It also has an antiseptic effect so people feel they are in a cleaner environment.

Blue and your body

The colour governs the thyroid and parathyroid glands. Blue is related to communication because it is linked to the throat area, and the upper lungs, arms and base of the skull. Visualize blue to dissolve fear of speaking up for yourself or if you are nervous about speaking in meetings. If you do experience these problems or have throat ailments, try wearing blue near your neck or wear a blue scarf. Use blue visualizations to increase your confidence when addressing a meeting, making a presentation or a wedding speech.

In China, blue was attributed to the dead and red to the living. This reflects the fact that the body of a dead person soon loses the warmth of life and takes on a bluish tinge. Similarly, if a person has a heart condition, his lips become blue because his blood is not sufficiently oxygenated to maintain all his organs. So, use blue visualizations to maintain or improve your circulatory system.

If you have a painful condition, it can help to visualize your pain or illness. You can do this literally so that you actually imagine your wrist throbbing with the pain of RSI (Repetitive Strain Injury), for example. Or you could see it symbolically as a dried out, creaking door hinge which rasps and grates as it changes position. Then see yourself healing the hurt or oiling that faulty hinge.

Blue light treatments

Blue light has been used for the treatment of jaundice in children. The whole body is exposed to the therapeutic rays and ultraviolet light encourages the skin to produce melanin, the tanning factor in our skin, and vitamin D. This helps our body to use calcium effectively so is useful in reducing inflammation caused by rheumatism and arthritis.

An experiment with Russian schoolchildren revealed that those who were exposed to additional invisible ultraviolet light appeared to grow faster, had fewer colds and produced better schoolwork. Of course, such experiments need to be repeated in order to discover just how widespread this phenomenon is, but such findings echo the earliest beliefs in the powerful properties of blue.

Exposure to blue light has been used in the treatment of premature babies where too much bilirubin is found in the blood. Physicians found that exposure to blue light was, in some cases, as beneficial as a complete blood transfusion.

Draw out your healing potential

It is a good idea to draw the site of your illness. This is not about artistic ability but about making internal feelings and knowledge external, to bring out what is hidden within.

Some people like to do a kind of x-ray picture which reveals the story below the surface. Others prefer to make an image of a symbolic creature, such as a snake, which constricts and chokes off their energy. Someone with RSI might draw a chain around their wrist, for example. Whatever your choice, it is right for you.

Your healing comes from your creativity and that is the most powerful assistance you can bring to the medical practitioners who treat you. Without your will to be healed they cannot help. All the medicine in the world will not make you better if you actively prevent improvement by choosing to stay ill. As you choose your images for healing you begin the process of empowering your journey to recovery.

If you are currently having treatment for illness, visualize it as being successful. Whether it is medically prescribed drugs, acupuncture or herbal treatment, if you believe it works then you make it work!

Visualize the glow of good health pouring into your body, with antiseptic blue neutralizing any infected or damaged tissue. Imagine yourself free of discomfort with no ill-health, and work towards seeing yourself blooming with new joy and energy.

Give yourself credit for the work you've done and the success you have had. Too often we don't give ourselves credit for the efforts we make or our achievements. However small the step you've taken, it is important to acknowledge it. Do this and you will be giving yourself the important message that you can and do make a difference to your own life.

HEALING CRYSTALS AND GEMSTONES

- **Aquamarine** – good for eyes, vision and clarity; enhances function of the nervous system and helps neuralgia.
- **Blue lace agate** – reduces anger and tension; increases effective communication; soothes inflammation.
- **Blue topaz** – encourages artistic growth; calms body and mind; aids concentration and meditation; good for leadership.
- **Blue tourmaline** – helps release blocked emotions; brings increased sense of peace and eases communication; good for throat.
- **Lapis lazuli** – a spiritual and aura cleanser; helps you gain wisdom and truth; good for strengthening friendships and for heart problems.
- **Sapphire** – promotes faith, friendship and love; boosts imagination and reduces nervousness; aids peace of mind.
- **Turquoise** – provides protection; increases confidence; develops friendship; aids intuitive awareness and meditation; good for throat problems such as laryngitis.

Diet Blues

You may find that you lose your appetite if you use a blue plate. Some weight loss programmes suggest you use blue dishes as an appetite suppressant or use blue light in food storage areas. In nature there are very few blue foods, apart from blueberries, so we do not automatically want to take this colour into our mouths. As a result, blue is more likely to put us off our food.

Psychologically, we are more likely to link blue to antiseptic properties – fine as a disinfectant but not as part of dinner. Also, deep in our most primitive brain, there lurks a primal memory that blue and black foods were likely to be poisonous or putrefying – again, not much of an appetizer. For the most part, those early colour warning signs are still with us.

Creative Visualization with Blue

The sapphire globe

This short visualization will help you to contact and confirm your own ability to protect yourself and those you love. You can use it daily before you get up.

First prepare yourself by relaxing, following the routine on pages 23–5.

> See yourself inside a sapphire-blue globe. It is as spacious as the inside of a hot-air balloon and as blue as the skies on a clear Mediterranean day. Into this globe you can invite anyone, person or animal, who you feel you love or is loving towards you – perhaps a partner, friends, a favourite dog or a neighbour. Imagine them coming in and settling around you in the peaceful space, surrounded by the clear blue that stretches to infinity.
>
> Allow the sapphire blueness to protect you by calling on it to encapsulate all who are gathered together in its inviolable blue light. It will accept only positive energy and keep out any harm that might befall you – that is the immunity it invites. Give thanks for this protection and watch those who entered the globe leave and, when you are ready, make your own departure into your waking world.
>
> If you do this every day on waking, you will prepare your mind for positive experiences and feel protected throughout the day. It need only take a minute or two and you can do it as you lie in bed!

Affirmations

- **I am open to the positive joys this day will bring.**
- **My life is protected and cherished.**
- **Protective peace surrounds me and those I love.**

Vase of wonder

In the colour wheel (see diagram on the inside front cover) the eight colours of the spectrum all occur opposite their complementary colour. Thus yellow is the complementary of violet, turquoise of red, and so on. In colour treatments, complementary colours are always used in order to maintain balance. In this short visualization, for relaxation, you will tune to the wonder of blue and its complementary colour, orange.

In your safe, comfortable space, prepare yourself by relaxing (pages 23–5).

Visualize in front of you, just beyond arms' reach, an exquisite blue vase. The blue is so intense you feel heady with the richness, like the purest sound you have ever heard or the freshest, most delicious fruit you have ever eaten.

Pause.

The vase is filled with orange lilies, orange sunflowers and all varieties of glowing orange flowers. Exquisite iridescent dragonflies, like threads from the sky, fly above the petals. The energy from the orange blooms and the blue vase reaches you, wrapping you in vibrations of calm energy.

Pause.

You feel a source of power rise within you. It has the clarity of ageless wisdom and the energy of growth. Together they harmonize and balance your body, mind and spirit. Feel the cooling rays of the blue reach into your body, soothing the stresses, whilst the zest of the orange creates joy. Feel the balance and notice how rested your body feels.

Affirmations

- **My guardian in wisdom is always with me.**
- **I have within me a wonderful undiscovered world which is revealed to me in every visualization.**
- **My body and mind work in perfect harmony.**

Time to reflect

Make a note of your feelings, any sensations that were particularly interesting and anything else that you think might be useful when you make a personal development plan in 'Sifting for Gold' in Chapter 10.

Creative Planting

> **In his blue garden, men and girls came and went like moths among the whisperings, and the champagne and the stars.**
>
> F Scott Fitzgerald, *The Great Gatsby*

The range of blue blooms is vast and you can absorb their powers by creating your own garden or by having blue flowers in your home. All you have to do is sit close to the flowers and focus your attention on them. Breathe in their fragrance and let the colour fill your imagination. Visualize the energy reaching into any part of your being in need of a cleansing treatment or some kind of clarification.

PLANTING SUGGESTIONS – ALL SHADES OF BLUE

Spring	Bluebells, forget-me-nots, *Pulmonaria*, *Clematis alpina*, primulas, grape hyacinths, Viola 'Azure Blue'.
Summer	*Meconopsis* (blue poppy), gentians, *Ageratum*, cornflowers, *Nigella*, *Ipomoea* 'Heavenly Blue', *Agapanthus*.
Autumn	Late-flowering *Ceanothus*, *Caryopteris*.

Personal Preferences

Blue has been a loved colour for thousands of years. Here are some recent praises:

TOTAL RELAXATION

Calm blue sea, soft music and fields of flowers come to mind as soon as I think of the colour blue. Thinking of these makes me feel calm, switches off my mind as if I am on holiday, lazing on a beach, reading and feeling totally relaxed. A turquoise sea lapping right next to me. The luxury of not working but letting the blue sky cover me and the sea refresh me, with no demands at all. Bliss.

Ellen

THE REAL ME

Orange contrasted with light blue gives me a sunny Mediterranean feel. Bright sunshine, warmth, relaxation with a touch of the exotic, the unexpected. This is another world away from all the cares and worries of everyday life, perhaps a fantasy world where I will see things and meet people that are new to me, triggering unexpected relationships, funny situations, relaxed carefree associations. Here is another country, an escape, but where I can be myself, my real me, creative, skilled, able to achieve my dreams. Not hampered or hindered by bureaucratic procedures, form filling, criticism and doubts. A land of music and rhythm.

Lyn

You can use the following pieces as short creative visualizations to introduce more of this colour into your system. Choose the one you like best, read through it and then close your eyes and imagine yourself bathed in the colour and its atmosphere.

ESSENCE OF LIFE

I have always liked the colour blue, probably because it is such a great part of life. The sky, the sea, is always there, visible. It has so many different shades, it can become almost white or almost green. It makes me feel peaceful. I like to sit outside on a warm sunny day and dream. I look up to the sky and just think of all the unexplored parts of the world that are out there waiting for me. I also have a favourite place. If I could choose where I'd like to live it would be by the sea, in a house overlooking the ocean. I dream of a desert island with a palm-fringed beach and white sand touching crystal clear, blue sea.

Many people find blue cold and depressing, but I feel only positive things from it. It is peaceful and even though the sky can turn dark or the sea can turn angry and treacherous, I still enjoy the effect and the colour. It will always pass and then the sky and the sea will return calm once more.

Daniel

PERFECT DAY

I like the colour blue because it reminds me of the sky on a beautiful summer's day. It makes me feel relaxed and happy because I associate it with holidays, relaxing, summer, sunshine, carefree days. Days when I feel free to do all the things I like, when I have time to read a book, go for a walk, swim, have a relaxing bath. Also, the colour reminds me of my wedding day: the bridesmaids wore blue. It was a perfect day – the sun shone all day and I was young and very, very happy and carefree. It also reminds me of blue hyacinths and bluebells in the woods when we would walk and run and play when I was a child.

Claudia

PEACE AND TRANQUILLITY

I remember blue skies meeting the sea in a magnificent, glorious blue. The sea is a calming influence, peaceful and tranquil. The sky powerful above, reflecting on the sea. A blue sky produces dramatic views, contrasting with the sun, reds and yellows. Blue is bold and strong. It has many shades. I feel I have the ability to think clearly with blue on – it is soothing.

Tom

VARIATIONS ON A THEME

There are so many shades and blends of blue that a whole book could be devoted to them. However, there is space for only a few here. For the rest, remember that whenever one colour is added to another their combined qualities must be taken into consideration as they will both have an effect.

Indigo

This shade governs the pituitary gland, which is 'the conductor of the orchestra', the controller of the endocrine system. Also, it represents the skeleton, particularly the spine. By working with this colour you get to the very structure of your life, beyond the superficial. So imagine indigo if you can't quite put your finger on what is wrong. Use it to get to the heart of your darkness.

Chakra Connection

Indigo is the colour of the Brow Chakra, which is linked to inner vision – the third eye – and is associated with pituitary gland. It allows us to develop spiritual wisdom and emotional growth. This chakra is the place to 'see through' situations and is the site of mysticism and psychic ability. It's where we get 'a bolt from the blue' inspiration from, in a 'blue flash'.

The Brow Chakra governs perception, intelligence and wisdom. From it we get a 'blueprint' for new ideas and designs. In its most developed, purest form it signifies infinite divine wisdom and enlightenment, which is why this colour is so often used in spiritual contexts. Through the Brow Chakra we can connect to the universe and to its creativity. This creative energy enables us to fulfil our life's purpose, to channel our vision beyond everyday reality.

Turquoise

Prized by Native Americans, Tibetans and Iranians for their mystical properties, turquoise stones have been used for millennia. In her book *Healing Quest* Marie Herbert explains how the Native Americans she journeyed with saw mining as a violation of the earth. They take only the silver or turquoise that is found above the surface. Both are worn for their protective qualities as well as their beauty.

One of the reasons turquoise is so highly valued is because it embodies the colours of sky and earth, so combining the spirituality of heaven and the groundedness of the land.

Like its neighbour pure blue, turquoise can be used to boost the immune system. Our immune defences depend mainly on the lymphatic system and turquoise helps to strengthen this. It also helps to reduce inflammation, thus making it a very good colour for treating infections, as Pauline Wills points out in *The Reflexology and Colour Therapy Workbook*.

Creative Visualization with Turquoise

Blue infinity

For this visualization it is preferable to lie flat. After following the relaxation technique (pages 23–5), you are ready to begin. Remember, at any time you can stop or go off and explore your own blue path.

reord

As you are resting, feel the support of the ground beneath your body. Be aware of the points where your body is supported and let your weight sink into the floor. As you breathe in let yourself feel the soft bed of pure white sand. It fits the contours of your body so that there is no part which is not held safely, no point through which stress cannot flow out.

As you open your eyes you find you are lying in a deserted clearing next to a vast expanse of turquoise water. Next to you there is a bright-blue tunic or breastplate with a gold design. This offers even more protection as well as truth. You may choose to wear either on your journey.

A kissing breeze keeps the temperature perfect for you. As you look out at the water, let in any sounds that rise to greet you. Perhaps you hear the lapping of the waves, the calling of sea birds, or the rhythmic slap of the water on rocks edging the shoreline.

Pause.

Smell the freshness of the water, feel the ions in the air cleansing your body, refuelling depleted energies. In this safe place you see the sky arching above you, stretching to infinity. An unending universe covers and protects you. As you look to the sky you feel yourself uplifted, rising without effort or fear into the wonder of cloudless blue infinity.

Pause.

Feel the rays of blue light cleanse you. Feel the tender turquoise rays soothing and boosting your immune system. As you float, secure in the knowledge there will be only gain from this flight, feel how you are building up an immunity to other people's negativity. The blue currents hold you. They empower your vision and create immunity from pain. Breathe in turquoise to counteract inflammation. Allow it to boost your immune system. Breathe out orange, its complementary colour.

Pause.

You are bathed in the clear insight of blue infinity. It connects you to the knowledge of the heavens, to the depths of the ageless seas. You feel at peace; any worries you may have come into perspective and no longer have the power to distress you. Change any sadness to a lightness of being. Your fears are only thoughts – let them melt into blue infinity.

Pause.

Back in your special clearing, you take off your blue and gold breastplate or tunic and lay it carefully in the place you found it. In future, if at any time you need its additional protection, you can visualize it and it will be there for you.

Feel yourself flooded with healing blue wisdom and take your attention back to the place where you are sitting or lying. When you are ready, stretch and return your attention to the room.

Affirmations

- **I am at one with the wisdom of the universe.**
- **I accept my potential and can create the life I want.**
- **My thoughts are clear and focused.**
- **I open myself to intuition and wisdom.**

Time to reflect

Make some notes to help you with your personal development plan in Chapter 10.

You may find that giving yourself symbolic protection, as with the blue and gold breastplate, adds security at times when you are threatened. Think about other blue strengths you could use: a royal blue cloak, a turquoise pendant, a belt made of sapphires. Visualize these to reduce your sense of vulnerability and enhance self-confidence.

Now is the time to leave the vastness of blue and travel through the natural wonder of a green landscape.

4

The Green Light

Keep a green tree in your heart and perhaps the singing bird will come.

CHINESE PROVERB

Green is made up of blue and yellow. Blue is in the first part of the cool side of the spectrum and yellow is at the opposite end on the magnetic hot side, so at midway in the spectrum, green is neither hot nor cold, passive nor active. It balances our negative and positive energies and soothes the mind, body and spirit.

Empowering Green

Working with green will empower you to new growth and love. This is the colour of the goddess Venus and of nature at her most fertile. It is the colour of hope, recovery and renewal and can be used to lift depressed *chi* (life force). (Suicides from Blackfriars Bridge in London dropped by 34 per cent after it was painted green.)

Green symbolizes the space our natural world gives us, a sympathetic sanctuary which reduces over-stimulation and brings stability. Green links us to love of the earth, regeneration and compassion, especially when we live with respect for nature and her laws. In Feng Shui terms, someone who lacks focus or whose mind drifts should wear green to ground them, to root them.

Mythical Connections

In the Egyptian *Book of the Dead*, the elaborate rituals surrounding death were described in great detail. The dead person had to be prepared for the journey to the other world, a journey that was every bit as important as any taken while he was alive. One part of the ritual involved a scarab of green stone which was placed on the chest of the deceased to 'open the mouth' and ensure his speech would be restored in his life beyond earth. This ritual symbolizes the renewal aspect of green.

Green was the colour the Egyptians painted their god Osiris, god of vegetation. And the floors of the temples of the Egyptian Pharoahs were often green to symbolize the fertile meadows of the Nile. As a kind of sympathetic magic it ensured that spring would return after winter and after the Nile flooded. The ancient Egyptians referred to time as 'the everlasting green one'.

Traditional winter celebrations, such as Christmas, connect us to rituals that have been followed for centuries, if not millennia. When we 'deck the halls with holly', ivy and pine trees, we symbolically show that though the year is at its darkest and all vegetation seems dead, new life awaits. It is an act of faith that new life will return – and part of the symbolic power of green.

Chakra Connection

Green is the colour of the Heart Chakra. The colour symbolizes gentle, natural growth suffused with nurturing love. The Heart Chakra is the centre of love and harmony. This is where your true self can shine through, and it is the point on the chakra path where the journey to higher consciousness and light truly begins.

This chakra covers the chest, shoulders and lower lungs. Imbalance here can lead to chest pains and heartache, as well as jealousy and envy. If your heart is closed, for whatever reason, your ability to receive love is impaired. When working on the Heart Chakra during visualization, try to open yourself to unconditional love. Green people are people with big hearts.

The spiritual path starts here, at the point where transpersonal knowledge is lodged, which is the connection point between our human dimension and our divine dimension – the Universal Consciousness, Gaia, Nature, God, or whatever name fits your experience of the spiritual aspect of your existence.

When there is a need for intense concentration on a complex mental task, then softer, cooler colours such as green reduce distraction. Breathe in green to concentrate and focus yourself, then breathe out magenta, its complementary colour, to complete the process. The use of green colour imagery enhances meditation and healing.

Healing with Green

Green is linked to the thymus gland, which is vitally important for a healthy immune system. Green too has antiseptic qualities so is very useful in cases of infection. In colour therapy, green light is used to destroy embryonic cell structure, which is particularly relevant in the treatment of cancer, but it should never be used if a woman is pregnant.

Healthy Colour Eating

Green foods have an abundance of chlorophyll, a nutrient that has been found to offset the effects of radiation, fight bacteria, detoxify the blood and speed the healing of wounds.

Dark-green vegetables such as spinach, broccoli, cabbage and Brussels sprouts are recommended for fighting off tumours and neutralizing carcinogens (for further details consult The *Optimum Nutrition Bible* by Patrick Holford). These greens are a good source of folic acid and are especially important for anyone planning to become pregnant, because folic acid is essential for healthy development of the foetus.

Creative Visualization with Nature (1)

The cycle of renewal

When you have been through your relaxation routine (pages 23–5), get ready to go on a journey which has four parts.

> As you inhale your next breath, imagine that you are bringing in light, filled with health-giving oxygen and the energy of the natural world, which are there to help you grow and renew yourself. As you breathe out, release any negativity and tiredness that is lodged in your heart.
>
> This is a journey to explore your Heart Chakra, the centre of your warmth and life force. With your next breath again feel yourself bringing in all the energy of the natural world, and let your attention go to the world in which you live. As you relax, let your mind go to a place in the heart of the countryside. See yourself in a place where natural growth and respect for nature

are key. Notice around you the rewards of hard work and a kind climate.

On this first part of your journey, you see beautiful fields of ripening corn, yellow and green and purple in their beauty, a rainbow of colours that nature puts together to delight the heart of the sun.

As you walk along the path you see a unique orchard in front of you, full of fruit trees from all corners of the earth. Look at the ripening, bright-green apples, luscious pears glistening pale-green and yellow in the freshness of the air, oranges reflecting the glow of the sun, and sharp and shiny limes. This is a place where you are welcome.

Reach up and take one of the apples. As you bite into it, feel the purity of the natural, unsprayed fruit. This is nature's bounty, uninterfered with in any way by processes that damage our natural world. Let the goodness of the apples feed your body as you walk on. Let the warmth of the day bathe your senses and recognize the natural order of the time when nature is putting on her show of glorious growth.

Pause.

This is the second part of your journey. Now the season has changed. The rich reds, oranges and golds of the leaves proclaim a change of season. Be aware of your feelings about this time of year; how do you feel now as the harvest is being gathered in, as the fruits of the fields are being collected?

Think about your own life and the harvests that you have made or are making at this moment. Do you feel that you are reaping the benefits of what you have sown? Or do you feel you should have sown more or perhaps different seeds? Are you harvesting what you need or what is best for you?

As you notice the rich abundance of the earth being brought in readiness for winter, take time to appreciate the glory of this season – the rich brown earth, the glorious autumn sky that stretches to infinity – and your place within it. You are a child of this universe and you too can enjoy the fruits of the earth.

Pause.

In this third part of your journey it is now winter. In the dark indigo sky you see stars. It's a diamond-studded sky, shining down on an earth that is getting ready to sleep and to renew its energies. The earth is covered with a protective blanket of snow. Reach down and touch the snow, feel its purity and its cold clarity. Beneath the snow lies dormant a whole new life force. Buried deep in the ground are seeds full of potential for renewal. These seeds, which are not visible now, will bring new life in the spring, but at the moment they are resting.

It is a time to conserve energy, to lie in the protective earth and take time. Think about your own life, do you need to stop and take time to renew your energies? Can you recognize that when it seems as if nothing is happening, as if everything is dead and finished, there is in fact another life in preparation, in waiting? How do you see your own life? Can you see a point in your life where to lie still and wait is exactly the right thing to do? Do you allow the seed that is within you the opportunity to rest before growth? You are a child of the universe and its cycles of rest are important to you too.

Pause.

In the final part of your journey, the earth is waking up. See yourself back in that beautiful countryside where you started, but this time nature is putting on her new clothes.

You see the bright green buds peeping through the trees around you, shimmering against the dark bark as they begin to wake from their slumbers to enter a new phase of their life, a new beginning.

Below your feet you can see the first shoots reaching out towards the sun that has warmed the earth ready for their arrival. All the cold and snow has disappeared and nature is in readiness for this, her new 'offspring', the new spring of life.

Be aware of renewed activity in the animals and birds around you. Look out for the fledglings as they begin their first adventures in the world of flight. Spring holds the promise of new growth, new possibilities and new harvests to come. It is a sign that nature does not die; instead, she allows time for rest, rebirth. The cycle of life never ends though it changes with the seasons.

Take your attention to your own life and the cycles that you have known. Where are you now in that cycle and how do you feel you express the point of growth in your life? Are you connected with the rhythm of the natural world? Do you nurture your potential for new growth and renewal? You are a child of nature and the cycle of your life is as important as that or every creature that exists on earth.

Reflect on how you need to nourish your wellbeing so that you can create your finest fruit, so that you too can shine in the sunlight that comes in spring, summer, autumn and winter. Perhaps too it is time to reflect that winter is not the end but one part of a replenishment cycle that keeps our life and the natural world in harmony and in growth.

Affirmations

- **The more I care for the earth, the more the earth nourishes me.**
- **My heart is open to the grace of love.**
- **Abundance is mine, I have only to reach out and take it.**

Time to reflect

Make some notes for yourself about the visualization so that you can look back at them when you get to Chapter 10, 'Sifting for Gold'.

The Healing Power of Nature

> **Variety of form and brilliancy of colour in the objects presented to patients are an actual means of recovery.**
>
> Florence Nightingale

Modern-day medicine is now starting to rediscover what has been known since earliest times. For instance, Galen, a second-century Greek physician, used to take his patients out into the local marketplace because he found it restored their spirits and enhanced their healing.

Nature has a soothing, restorative effect on humans. In Robert Ulrich's Study, 'Effects of Interior Design on Wellness', it is reported that patients who can look at a picture of the natural world from their hospital bed tend to recover faster than those who look at a blank white wall. And that those whose rooms look out on trees often have shorter hospital stays, make fewer negative comments and need fewer painkillers than patients who stare at blank, boring spaces.

Where people are recovering from serious illness, interacting with nature helps renew their sense of hope and coherence. It's a form of natural meditation. Healing gardens are now being designed for specific issues; these can be in atriums or greenhouses, they do not have to be huge formal gardens. When designing a garden for Alzheimer's patients, for example, where a sense of safety and familiarity is needed, Japanese-inspired designs with their sense of order and scale are preferable.

Working with plants in a greenhouse setting has proved to be powerful medicine for patients with mental or emotional problems. The act of growing and tending to living things can give a sense of purpose and order and ease a troubled outlook. For those coping with devastating emotional issues, the garden needs to feel particularly safe and soothing – no looming plants or surprises. People recovering from disfiguring illnesses benefit from gardens with more 'private' areas.

'Sick Building Syndrome' is not confined to offices; our homes also carry potentially damaging pollutants. To get rid of these harmful, invisible nasties, help is at hand in the form of green plants, especially if you have got green fingers. Certain houseplants act as natural indoor air-filters, cleansing the air of common irritants like carbon monoxide and formaldehyde. Particularly effective plants are Chinese evergreen, mother-in-law's tongue, philodendron, ferns, spider plants and indoor figs. These are mostly low-maintenance and need only occasional watering when the soil starts to dries out.

Gardener's delight

> **All theory, dear friend, is grey, but the golden tree of actual life springs ever green.**
>
> Goethe, *Faust*

When you work in the garden you absorb the healing properties of nature through your eyes and skin.

The birthday of Japanese Emperor Hirohito is celebrated as 'Green Day' because he cherished his garden so much. Like many before and since, he understood the healing space that gardens offer.

Herbs are particularly soothing: camomile calms nerves, comfrey soothes bruised limbs, feverfew eases headaches and peppermint helps digestion. At present, of 25 top-selling pharmaceutical drugs, half have their origins in plants.

HEALING CRYSTALS AND GEMSTONES

- **Aventurine** – helps with hypertension, migraine and insomnia; increases vitality.
- **Chrysoprase** – eases sorrow; beneficial for the ovaries in women, the prostate and testicles in men; improves thyroid function; increases optimism.
- **Emeralds** – the gemstone of prophecy; helps with insomnia; develops the intellect and anything related to love.
- **Green calcite** – increases awareness and intuition; improves pancreas function.
- **Green tourmaline** – good for grounding and restabilizing after an upset; helps regulate blood pressure; aids inspiration.
- **Jade** – helps with eyes and vision; increases wisdom; improves bladder problems and kidney function.
- **Malachite** – encourages healthy eyesight; wards off negative vibrations, invites happiness.
- **Peridot** – restores emotional balance; good for vision; helpful for insomnia and the nervous system generally; a good tonic; possesses occult powers.

Creative Visualization with Nature (2)

From the heart

After your relaxation (see pages 23–5), find your way to your special clearing, the place where you feel secure and protected, where you can bathe in the warmth of the day whilst the gentle breeze caresses your body. Today you are going to explore an area you have not yet ventured into.

Just out of reach behind some trees you can see a hill rising in the distance. It is covered in the new spring grass. When you are ready, get up and make your way towards this hilly area. Be aware of the sounds of the birds and notice a sense of confidence as you walk out from your special clearing towards a new point of exploration.

Pause.

As you walk, you see that the path is rising slightly, that the ground beneath your feet is gently sloping upwards. You come past the trees and can see there is a path which has been used by others in the past. Though not well trodden, it is clearly a path that is used regularly, although at the moment you cannot see anyone else.

Around you the valley rises. As you walk along the path you feel the strength in your body to explore and the desire in your mind to understand new concepts and to know more about the truth that lies in the heart of you. Enjoy the feeling of peace and tranquillity that comes to you, tinged with an edge of excitement as you realize that new possibilities are ever present.

Pause.

As you walk you see a spring to your left. It is a natural spring, a fountain at the side of the path, and as you get closer you notice crystal water bubbling into a rocky basin which then seems to dip underground. You stop and cup your hands to collect some water to drink. This water has the power to feed your body and soul. It tastes like no water you have ever had before; it fills every part of your being with light and hope and renews the very essence of your being.

Pause.

As you look up after taking a final drink of water, you notice just below a little grotto by the side of the path. This grotto was not visible before but anybody who drinks at this life-giving point, must see it, but only if they drink.

Make your way to the grotto; it is full of signs of hope and new beginnings. Look at what you can see in the grotto. People have been there before and placed many objects in it: there are fresh flowers – beautiful green-stemmed pink roses; there is a tiny Buddha figure on a green mat; there is a cross; there is a painting of a lotus flower, pale-green leaves at the bottom and rosy-pink petals at the top – the symbol of the Heart Chakra. And somebody has placed a ring there too, a golden ring, the symbol of eternity, of the unending cycle of life.

Pause.

This is a place where people come to make pledges and to ask for their heart's desire. It is a place that not everybody knows about, but you have found it. Now is the time for you to make your request, if you wish to. In this time of green renewal you can make a request to enable you to find new directions, new hopes, new beginnings, because you are a child of nature and as such, renewal is part of your cycle of life.

Pause.

Take some time to think about what you would wish to say and make your own offering; give whatever you feel is most appropriate at this point in time. Give it from the heart and in return you will receive abundance in your heart.

Pause.

Spend some time reflecting on this most beautiful secret grotto you have discovered. When you are ready, make your way back to your space in the clearing and feel the warmth and security of this special place. Then take yourself back to the room in which you are sitting or lying. Recognize the sense of renewal that has entered your whole being. Feel the green of hope that stays in your heart, tinged with the pink of unconditional love. You are a loved child of the universe, your place is secure.

Affirmations

- **Everything I desire now comes to me.**
- **I am one with the Universal Spirit and see only completion.**
- **I live in a place of rich variety and see clearly its meaning in my life.**

Time to reflect
Make some notes about your experience for the exploration that will come later.

Personal Preferences

ABUNDANCE

Leaves above wet grass,
Palm trees stretching to infinity.
Limes filled with sharp abundance,
Stones of emerald in unlimited expanse.
Green is my colour;
I smell fresh, dark mint,
I taste green broccoli,
I hear bamboo woodchimes
And smell the dark secrets of pine woods.
Nature's abundance,
My inheritance.

MV

LUSH GREEN GRASS

A field of lush green grass billowing in the wind and undulating down to the water. Smell of freshness and a vision of open space. A cool summer's morning. Expectations of the day ahead. A feeling of contentment and inner peace. A sense of satisfaction, completeness and fulfilment. Alone but not lonely. Natural, soothing and peaceful.

Helen

Creative Visualization with Nature (3)

Mountain path companion

Once you are fully relaxed (see page 5), allow yourself to explore the empowering experience of another colour visualization.

As you breathe in you find yourself on a mountain ridge, on a wide path studded with clumps of wild camomile. Green agates sparkle in the afternoon light. You see spread in front of you a wide cultivated plain where every shade of green glows. Notice the green of the olive groves, see the rich greens of the lime trees, their dark leaves glistening with recent rain drops. As you smell the fresh citrus aroma, let the energy of the emerald fields reach up to you and the dark green of the cypress trees soothe you.

You are protected by your higher consciousness and your vantage point lets you view your life from a higher perspective. Take the time to sit and rest. Look at your surroundings. What else do you notice? Touch the green agates. How do they feel? What do they offer to you? If you are anxious, pick a bunch of camomile; it calms nerves and will steady you in your exploration.

Pause.

You feel a sense of calm courage flooding your body. Notice that energy strengthening your being, giving you bravery and power. As you sit you see an animal coming towards you. It offers no harm. Instead it carries to you knowledge of the natural way to be in the world. Allow it to come closer, knowing it holds great significance for you.

Take your time to greet the animal. Look at it closely? What size is it? How does its fur feel? Stroke it and allow yourself to respond to the warmth it brings to you. Is it like any other animal you have ever known? What spirit of nature does it carry? Lions have courage, dogs have devotion, owls have wisdom. What do you feel your animal symbolizes for you?

Pause.

Sit with this animal who is totally at one with the natural world.

Be aware of the steady beauty of your heartbeat, the quiet breathing as you wait in anticipation, for the creature has something for you. It might be a message that comes from looking into each other's eyes, it might be something carried in the pelt of the animal, or it might be a natural object which your attention is drawn to by the animal. Perhaps it is something to help you become more decisive. Perhaps it will help you to grow through your fears. Perhaps it is courage in the form of a piece of bark which will protect you, or a cloak of shimmering green light that will keep you safe whilst it dazzles that which you fear. Perhaps it is a seed to give you the opportunity to grow once more.

Whatever you receive, it is significant for your personal growth. Hold it, examine it closely and lovingly and look into the eyes of the giver once more. What is there that you could learn? Repeat the answer to yourself and hold whatever it is in your heart.

Pause.

Offer your thanks to this wise one who has shared nature's wisdom with you. Give heart-felt thanks and take your leave, remembering you can come back at any time you choose.

Make your way back along the path secure in the knowledge that you are protected and have made connection with a vitally important part of your own natural being.

Time to reflect

When you are ready, reflect on your visualization and make some notes to help you when you sift for gold. Drawing a picture of the animal you met would be very helpful.

VARIATION ON A THEME

Olive Green

Olive green has traditionally been a symbol of peace, ever since the dove brought back the olive branch to Noah's ark after the flood. Olive green is also symbolic of light, because olive oil was used as fuel in lamps. And this particular shade of green symbolizes transmutation – the change from one form to another – because olives cannot be eaten straight from the tree but must first undergo a chemical process. Olive green symbolizes feminine leadership qualities with the added dimension of heart qualities.

The last anointing with oil, originally probably olive oil, is a symbol of death and rebirth, and because of this olive green is the colour of harmony and completion. In addition, the Mount of Olives was a sacred place of power for Jesus and his disciples.

You can use olive green in your creative visualizations when you want to bring about a change from disturbance to tranquillity, especially when you want to heal friction in relationships. Choose a serene setting in a landscape that you know; imagine yourself sitting there and allow yourself to be surrounded by soothing rays of olive green. The olive green changes to the white light of illumination which enables your intuition to reveal how you can most effectively, and safely, make the changes you need. The healing peace of olive green will be your guide.

Now we must leave the natural power of green to explore the glowing glory that is yellow.

5

Yellow: Sunshine for Sensuous Success

A sun. A light that for want of a better word I can only call yellow. Pale sulphur yellow, pale lemon gold. How beautiful yellow is!

VINCENT VAN GOGH

Yellow stands next to white in terms of brightness. It is the colour of the sun at its most intense, of the sun which comes from the darkness and returns to darkness once its visible cycle is over. Yellow also typifies light, but it does not have the same intense purity as white light.

Yellow symbolizes the divine love which enlightens human awareness and understanding (in some Christian services, yellow is used as an alternative to white). It is also the emblem of gold, the noblest of metals. In China, yellow is the imperial colour.

Clever Yellow

Yellow is the colour of learning as well as intuition because, like the sun, yellow brings flashes of inspiration and wisdom. It's good for revealing the sources of conflict or distress and for unravelling mysteries. Yellow gets to the core of the matter by penetrating the deepest, darkest levels. Yellow is associated with the bright shining light of clarity – you can't hide from that bright torch which illuminates every hidden place.

This is the symbol of the mind, intellect, wisdom and problem solving. Yellow is stimulating. It strengthens the nerves and improves mental ability; it encourages clear and positive thinking. It also brings detachment. Sometimes, though, thinking too much may make you procrastinate; if so try adding a little of the energy of red to strengthen your resolve to carry out your task. The Buddha's colour is yellow, or gold, but when he meditated on the harsher aspects of the human condition, he wore red robes. Red acts as a grounding colour and gives more heart energy.

In its negative aspect yellow signifies meanness, treason, deceit and cowardice. A 'yellow streak' in someone implies they are faint hearted and lack courage. It reflects a degree of jealousy, lack of trust and fear.

Points of transition

Yellow on traffic lights cautions us to wait; it is a transition point between stop and go. A yellow flag signifies quarantine, again an interim phase where a cessation or waiting time is required, as at amber traffic signals. Yellow also connects; it is the colour of networking. When you pause to review your life, visualize yourself bathed in yellow light for insight and to show connections to others who might help you. Remember, when you need a teacher one will come into your life. Be open to the possibility.

Mythical Connections

Yellow is the colour of Athena, goddess of wisdom and patroness of institutions, learning and the arts. Invoking her support will add to your sense of confidence, and if you include a yellow item in a visualization, its vibrations will act as a psychological connection to feelings of positive power. Athena's robes were golden, to signal her wisdom. Yellow is the colour of the mind and acquired learning, so if you are studying it is particularly helpful.

The ancient Greeks believed that the colour of the robes of the gods and goddesses symbolized their achievements; their robes were an outer sign of their powers that was clearly visible for all to see, much as the ceremonial robes of today's leaders are.

Chakra Connection

It is significant that the colour for the Solar Plexus Chakra is yellow, the brightest colour in the spectrum and the colour which holds the most light. Energy is drawn in through the solar plexus and distributed to all the other chakras, which is one reason why this centre is sometimes called 'the psychic energy pump'. The endocrine gland found at this chakra level is the pancreas.

This is the chakra that links us to creativity, wellbeing, pleasure and abundance. When we bring energy into this chakra, either through meditation or visualization, it will revitalize us and allow us to experience the warmth and enjoyment of physical activities.

The Solar Plexus Chakra is your personal sun, the fire in your belly and your place of empowerment. It is the sun (hence 'solar') that has descended into your nervous system. It is the centre of self-worth. Whatever in your life has not been sorted out, lingers here, with the potential to create stress.

Sometimes people who focus on this chakra put all their energy into physical activities and have difficulty raising their attention to more spiritual matters. If this is the case for you, you may need to visualize with yellow's complementary colour, which is violet.

This chakra relates to the liver, the gall bladder, spleen and stomach. It is particularly concerned with digestive functions and is helpful in all the stimulation and elimination processes of the body. It also helps get rid of calcium and lime deposits which can form in the gall bladder and kidneys giving rise to gall or kidney stones.

Healing with Yellow

Yellow is the eliminator, the toxic waste treater. It helps get rid of what you don't need, so visualize yellow when you want to rid yourself of any waste. Eliminating what is no longer useful is a law of nature. If you hold on to things for too long after they have fulfilled their purpose, they can only decay. Once they become contaminated, if they are not released, they taint what is right next to them. Problems with elimination cause disease: prostate problems, bladder infections, constipation and, in psychological terms, holding onto the past, not letting go.

Where 'gut feelings' are denied, where emotions are repressed rather than expressed, physical and mental disorders follow. In anorexia, for example, gut feelings are not acknowledged and dealt with to the point that the person literally cannot stomach nourishment. When things go wrong with the liver and gall bladder, we may develop jaundice and our skin turn yellow; liver disease also has this effect. In Germany in the Middle Ages, yellow turnips and yellow spiders rolled in butter were used as cures.

'Sympathetic magic', a precursor of scientific treatments, was used in India as a cure for jaundice. In the sick room, yellow objects were gathered to extract the yellow from the patient and then red objects, such as the hair of a red bull, were brought in to encourage a red, healthy glow.

In ancient China a patient with disease of the colon would be covered in yellow paint and surrounded by yellow light to drive out the cramps that were a symptom of the disorder. In Chinese medicine, yellow represents the earth.

Yellow tones and cleanses the system and promotes the flow of gastric juices which aid digestion. It generates energy in the muscles. Any part of the body that lacks energy can be treated with this colour. It works well with the skin, cleansing and healing scars and eczema. According to Theo Gimbel, using yellow in colour therapy relieves arthritic pain by dissolving the calcium deposits in the joints.

Yellow is also helpful in loosening and getting rid of colds. Hot lemon drinks help eliminate toxins by flushing out the system. Lemon and yellow invigorate and cleanse the body. Yellow has also been found to raise low blood pressure associated with anaemia.

Energy booster

If you find yourself flagging during the day, put something yellow – such as a vase of bright-yellow chrysanthemums – nearby. Research shows that yellow has a positive effect on the mind and an energizing effect on the body. Daffodils, sunflowers, yellow roses and laburnum will also do the trick.

Another quick colour visualization is to imagine you are drinking in the golden yellow rays of the sun. Tilt your head back and feel the clarity of its illumination filling your whole being, eliminating all that is past its sell by date. Fill your mind with the glow of yellow light then witness it sweeping your digestive system free of the unwanted waste that lodges there.

HEALING CRYSTALS AND GEMSTONES

- **Amber** – enhances bladder function; good for intestinal disorders and nervous-system problems; eases rheumatism; helpful for sore throats.
- **Beryl** – helps heart conditions; useful in mental-health disorders; an aid to self-knowledge; good for mouth and throat infections.
- **Citrine** – helpful for depression and finding one's direction in life; induces dreams; benefits stomach problems.
- **Carnelian** – helpful during menstruation; eases neuralgia; clarifies thought; strengthens voice.

- **Jasper** – a blood cleanser; helps digestive function; good for a troubled mind and the nervous system; steadies pulse.
- **Mimetite** – enhances communication skills.
- **Tiger's eye** – good for asthma; increases self-confidence and insight; helpful in psychosomatic illnesses.
- **Topaz** – helpful in intellectual pursuits and psychic development; calms the body so useful for nervous-system problems, insomnia and stress; improves blood circulation; helps in colds and flu.
- **Yellow jade** – aids digestion; increases intuition.

Healthy Colour Eating

Yellow foods are good for a well-functioning bladder and bowels because of yellow's association with elimination. Citrus fruits – oranges, lemons and grapefruits – both stimulate us and aid with toxic disposal. If you have orange or grapefruit juice or water with lemon first thing in the morning, it will flush out any material stuck in the gut and colon, which is very important if you want to enhance bowel function. Visualize the flow of cleansing fluids through your system.

Fruit contains essence of sunshine. Also, the less these are cooked, the better, since many minerals and vitamins are destroyed in the cooking process. Eat yellow pulses, lentils and beans, or tofu to ensure you have protein, as well as eggs, perhaps 'sunny side up'. Enjoy bananas and pears and yellow mirabelle plums when in season. Eat apricots, honeydew melon, star fruit and pineapples as well as the citrus fruits already mentioned. The sharp freshness of lemons will add zest to your life but try to ensure it does not make you acidic and sharp tongued.

Deep-yellow and orange vegetables such as sweet potatoes, peppers, yellow tomatoes, sweetcorn and carrots are high in betacarotene and other antioxidants which help to protect healthy cells from free radicals – unstable and potentially damaging molecules that could harm your DNA.

Creative Visualization with Yellow (1)

To a new shore

To increase the power of this visualization you can include yellow somewhere – in your clothes, your surroundings, or the pen and paper you later use to write your record. This yellow journey is bathed in fulfilment and warmth. On this journey you will find that you have everything that you need; if it is not with you now, it will be given to you on the way. First prepare yourself by relaxing (see pages 23–5).

Imagine that you are getting up from the place where you now sit or lie, and are travelling to a place, a clearing in a forest, that lies beside a river. Be aware when you arrive there of the soft grass beneath your feet, the trees that allow yellow sunlight to come through to your clearing, and the smell of healthy plants warmed by the sun.

Find a place to sit in the clearing where you feel comfortable and perfectly safe. Once you are settled look out towards the river. Look carefully at the river; is it surging along or flowing quietly and smoothly? Can you see any life in the river? Is it muddy or clear? Really allow your gaze to move with the flow of the river, taking in all its many changes.

Pause.

Be aware of your feelings towards the river. Does it make you feel comfortable, nervous, a little frightened? Does it look inviting? Would you like to go into the river and perhaps swim or float along? As you sit in your bright dappled space be aware of any sounds around you, the sounds of birds or perhaps the rustle of leaves. Feel the warm sun caress your neck and shoulders.

You decide that you want to go across the river, so make your way to the bank and look up and down for a place to cross. Perhaps there is a bridge, maybe there is a boat. If you wish you can wade across or swim to the other side. Choose whichever way feels best for you – you have the knowledge within you to make the right choice. Remember, if at any time you decide that this is not for you, you can stay where you are or take your attention elsewhere and just relax in the space that you find yourself in.

Pause.

As you are crossing the river, notice the depth. How do you

feel about this? Is there anybody there to help you? Would you welcome assistance or do you feel completely secure with the task that you have undertaken? Feel the water on your skin, taste the clarity on your tongue. Your senses quiver with anticipation.

Once you have reached the other side of the river, stop and take a rest. Be aware of any changes in your environment. Is there is anything unusual here? Do you notice any people, animals, plants, or more unusual creatures or objects? Is this a very different place from the grassy warm forest that you left? Whatever you see holds the potential for increased wisdom for you. Acknowledge all sensations and sights and store them in your memory.

Pause.

A little way ahead you notice a building bathed in sumptuous shades of yellow, from pale primrose to glowing saffron. This building holds special importance for you. Feeling secure and at ease, you make your way towards that building. Feel the path or the ground underneath your feet. Be aware of any sensations on your skin, any sounds, or any aromas in the air. Let your senses be open to all that is available to you in this special place. You are flooded with sensuous pleasure.

As you get closer to the building, notice how it is constructed. What material is it made out of? Does it have a roof? What are the walls like? Is there anything special or unusual about this building?

Pause.

You see a doorway and the entrance is clear for you to go in. This is a place that holds significance for you. You are expected there and are welcome. You will gain important knowledge there, to help you develop both your sensual nature and your mental abilities. Once you go through the entrance way you notice a person in the interior. This might be a person you know or it might be a person from another time or place, or a person who is not readily identified by you. Notice how he or she is dressed. The person has a gift for you and means only to help you on your journey through life. Look into his or her eyes. What message is being communicated? What words do the eyes speak? How can these words help you on your life path?

Pause.

You go closer to the person who has waited for you, waited for you with a gift, and notice that you are being given something that has been kept especially for you. Your whole being is tingling with energy, pulsing with vital life force.

Take the gift and examine it. Is it wrapped? If so, what is the wrapping like? What colour is it? You are now holding the gift, and you have opened the wrapping. Look at it carefully. What do you see? Is it something you have always wanted? Does this person say anything?

Pause.

Perhaps you do not understand that it is a present; perhaps it does not feel like a gift but something ordinary, not at all special. Whatever the gift is, its importance to you at this point is certain. Later you can think about it in more detail; for the moment accept it and thank the benefactor.

Is there something that you want to ask this person? You may want further information or perhaps you want an affirmation. If there is anything that you need to say, speak now because quite soon you will be leaving to return to your safe place.

Pause.

You now have to decide whether you want to bring the gift back with you or leave it there. Now you have found this building you will be able to return there whenever you do this visualization – this is your special place beyond the river. At any time you can go there in your imagination. For now, decide to either leave the gift – in which case place it somewhere that feels appropriate – or take it with you.

It is time to say goodbye to the person. Take one last look around the space in which you found yourself and make your way back towards the door through which you came. Leave the building and move back towards the river, all the time being aware of the ground beneath your feet, the air on your skin, the warmth of the sun caressing your neck and shoulders. You can see in front of you the river waiting for you to re-cross. Make your way back towards the opposite shore, back to your place in the clearing.

When you arrive there, sit down and take time to reflect and feel the warm security of your special safe clearing. Be aware of the journey that you have just made, the gift that you were given and any unusual things that happened to you. Be aware that these came from your inner wisdom and knowledge in order to give you information.

Pause.

Allow yourself to bathe in the warm yellow glow from the sun and reflected yellow light. It surrounds you with security and an energy as brilliant as diamond starbursts.

Now make the journey from your clearing back to the room in which you are sitting or lying. Be aware of your weight on the chair or the floor. Feel the support that you are being given. Let your attention return to your body and feel the air in the room, be aware of the temperature in the room and any noises or sounds in the background. Notice your breathing and feel yourself back in the spot where you began your journey.

When you are ready, open your eyes. It is a good idea at this point to stretch towards the ceiling and then to relax once more. Do not get up straight away, but take a few minutes to think about your journey. Be aware of how you feel now and think about the events that took place.

Time to reflect

If you want to use these colour visualizations as part of a personal development journey, make some notes about the experience. Perhaps make a note of the gift you received, and write short descriptions of any people that you met, and the landscape. Make notes of the building you were in and anything else that felt unusual.

Pay attention to any colours or sensations that you had and again jot these down.

For the moment, take time to reflect on anything that you have learnt from this journey – perhaps the message that you got from the person's eyes or from the words that were spoken. However this message was communicated to you, it is important to try and understand it and to accept its value. If at the moment it seems to hold no sense for you, then record it so you can work on it later.

Sometimes we do not understand our inner guides and wisdom straightaway; we need time to nurture them just as seeds need to be nurtured so that they gain strength to grow from darkness towards the golden illumination of the sun.

A perfect path of the Truth has come into being for our journey to the other shore beyond the darkness.

Rig Veda, 1.93.4.

Short visualizations

Your powers of colour visualization can be increased by engaging in short visualizations. You do not have to spend a long time going through your relaxation procedure, though it might help. All you need to do is choose one of the titles from the list below and close your eyes. Whilst you do that let your mind fill with the images, sensations, sounds, textures, tastes and aromas that are evoked by contemplating the subject. Let your imagination have free rein and allow the colour of yellow to permeate the scene.

Your visualizations can be as short or as long as you want them to be, and you may find that unobtrusive music is helpful with the process. Remember, you are in charge and you can do whatever you need to do in order to develop your ability in creative colour visualization.

- The rays of the sun in a stained-glass window.
- A ripe wheatfield in summer sunshine.
- The golden yellow of sunflowers.
- The yellow glow of molten metal.
- A sunset over the sea.

Creative Planting

Use yellow to bring sunshine into your garden and home all year round.

PLANTING SUGGESTIONS – FROM PALE CREAMS TO BRIGHT MUSTARDS

Spring	Laburnum, *Michelia figo* (an evergreen shrub with banana-scented, creamy-yellow flowers), rhododendrons and azaleas in shades of yellow, forsythia, *Mahonia* 'Charity', daffodils, primroses and crocuses, mimosa.
Summer	*Acer japonicum* 'Aureum', creamy hypericums and potentillas.
Autumn	*Cassia didymobotrya* ('Golden wonder').
Winter	*Pyracantha* 'Golden Dome', winter jasmine, variegated ivy.

Creative Visualization with Yellow (2)

My sweetness

This visualization will help bring energy and vitality to the Solar Plexus Chakra, so aim to take your attention there. It is a place where we often feel nauseous and churned or knotted up.

The Sanskrit word for this chakra, *Swadisthana*, means 'my home' or 'my sweetness'. Think of this as you bring in the power of yellow. This is a safe place where you can be at home with yourself; re-discover the home that is within you – and what a safe and nourishing place this can be. As you become more and more filled with the radiating warmth, feel yourself being more centred, more grounded, connected to home.

In your comfortable, safe place, go through your usual relaxation routine (see pages 23–5).

On an in-breath, imagine that you are taking in the energy of warm yellow lights. Imagine a small circle being filled with the warmth of yellow and orange, and as you breathe vitality into this area, imagine it radiating further and further out from the centre.

The golden yellow in the area of your stomach is filled with energy and bright power, a power that will help you to increase your feelings of self-love and self-respect and find a new appreciation of your own worth.

In the past your feelings of self-worth may have been damaged; energy may have been drained away from your sense of self so that at times you may have felt that you had lost sight of who you were, what you were doing and the meaning of your life. If these feelings disturb you still, this is your opportunity to revitalize that part of you which is central to your wellbeing.

Pause.

Take a deep breath, and as you breathe in, feel the warmth of the sphere glowing and spreading. As it does so, it is spreading the belief in your ability to achieve happiness and wellbeing and to eliminate negativity and self-harm. As the yellow light detoxifies the organs in this area, it leaves room for beneficial light and love to filter in, filling up the space left created by the departure of negativity.

Pause.

Once you visualize the yellow and orange light radiating from the point just below your navel, spread the colour throughout this whole area of your body. See the yellow transformed into a light that moves through your pelvis into your intestines, bladder and kidneys, and all of the organs in this part of the body. See the glow flowing through, flushing away all the inflammation, disease, anxiety and tension that is lodged in these areas. As it is swept away, feel the great sense of wholeness and wellbeing that is left in its place.

Pause.

You can let the wonderful experience of contented pleasure rise and spread through the rest of your body as well. Just remember to breathe regularly and with each breath take the yellow and orange glow further into the other organs of your body.

Pause.

As you sit or lie in your comfortable safe place and feel the glow spreading through your body, allow yourself to fill with a sense of abundance, a feeling of prosperity. Be aware of the fact that you already have everything that you need to make yourself well, happy and fulfilled. You have the power to bring the sweetness of life and love to your life; like the yellow and orange glow permeating the whole of your body, that feeling of harmony and wellbeing can encompass all aspects of your life. Whatever you have is nourishing.

Pause.

Feelings of self-worth are not dependent on what you achieve in the outside world, how much money you earn, or any of the material aspects of life that are so time-consuming. You can appreciate the wonder of who you are just by accepting your unique value as a human being. You are a wonderful person simply because you are here and are who you are. Welcome.

The currents of the Universal Being circulate through me;
I am part of God.

Waldo Emerson

Affirmations

- **I give myself permission to shine.**
- **All obstacles dissolve, leaving my path clear for success.**

Personal Preferences

GLOWING FROM THE INSIDE

This colour reminds me of the sun and its warmth. It makes me feel happy and alive. I feel full of energy and am glowing from the inside. I am on a beach relaxing, strolling through the sand and at the edge of the water. I am very happy and can stay here forever.

Gina

OPTIMISTIC YELLOW

Sun, brightness, life, daisies, sunflowers, sunrays, sunshine, warmth, fire, happiness, hope, optimism, holidays, daylight, sunlight, sand.

Wendy

We now leave the brilliant warmth of yellow for the majesty of purple.

6

Power of Purple

Majestic Purple

Before chemical dyes were invented, the colour purple was wondrously rare. The dye known as Tyrian purple was obtained from molluscs of the genus *Murex*, but it was a difficult, painstaking process, and a costly one, so purple clothes were highly desired and worn only by those with the rank to afford them. Purple was an exclusive colour, out of the reach of all but the wealthiest.

'Born to the purple' signified royal birth and was the colour worn by Roman Emperors. Similarly, in heraldry, purple or 'murrey' represents royalty or rank. Today it is still the distinctive colour of leaders and imperial sovereignty.

Purple is made up of blue, which symbolizes devotion, and red, which denotes passion. It is therefore a union of spirit and body, love and wisdom. In Judaism the holy colours are red, blue, purple and white. Purple is the peacemaker between the old and the new.

The Spiritual Connection

If you have ever asked Who am I? Where am I going? What is the meaning of my life? or What happens after death? then you probably feel a need to develop the spiritual aspect of yourself.

The spiritual understanding of life is a life-long quest. The crown chakra connects you with the universal spirit, or whichever spiritual being you believe in. Those involved in any kind of spiritual journey find that with continued meditation, prayer or yoga practice this chakra becomes more open and developed. Enlightened beings such as gurus, mystics, shamans or spiritual leaders focus energy on this, the crowning chakra. It is hardly surprising that in many traditions purple is the colour of the visionary.

We can develop our self-esteem, find inner peace and wellbeing and discover a path that leads to happiness by working on this aspect of life. Those who are on a spiritual quest recognize that life throws into our path situations which enable us to learn and grow. Each event, however upsetting, provides a lesson that gives us the chance to open up to the greater meaning of our existence.

Mythical Connections

The purple robes worn by the legendary Ulysses on his mythical journey, recorded in *The Odyssey*, symbolized his sea wanderings and his power to triumph over whatever dangers came his way. The ancient Egyptians carried a purple amulet to ward off adversity.

Healing with Purple

When spiritual energy is repressed, there is an increased likelihood of stress-related illnesses, skin rashes, nervousness and emotional disturbance. The fact that the mind and body are out of balance when this aspect is denied, means that part of you will constantly seek spiritual sustenance. If this need is repeatedly ignored, then the body will in some way make its distress known. Serious illness is frequently the call to 'wake up' and change damaging patterns of living.

Purple colour visualizations will help you distance yourself from personal and material preoccupations and dispel those threatening memories that stalk you, the ones that hold on even when you have tried to work them through. Obsessively remembering and replaying negative events succeeds only in fixing them more firmly in your memory, so it is important to let them go. The visualizations in this chapter will strengthen your ability to free yourself from bonds of addiction and despair.

Purple is good for mental and nervous problems, though if there is a history of depression or suicidal behaviour too much purple may depress a person even further so is best avoided. Too much purple can be ungrounding, but in moderation it is useful to calm erratic emotions. Purple combines the stimulating effect of red with the tonic effect of blue.

Successful surgery

If you have to go into hospital for an operation the more relaxed and well-informed you are the more likely it is that your surgery will be successful and your recovery time reduced. Because the more you do to help yourself the better you will feel, use colour as part of your healing plan.

One way to lower pre-operative stress is colour healing visualization. Envision yourself in the operating theatre feeling calm, secure in the knowledge that all is well. Mentally see yourself helping the surgeon by keeping any incision free of infection, by maintaining normal blood pressure and by keeping bleeding, pain and discomfort to an absolute minimum. See yourself surrounded by cleansing blue light, with purple at the top of your head flooding your mind with the wisdom of generations of healers.

After your operation, use colour visualization to speed up recovery by bathing the affected area with whatever colour you feel will be most beneficial. On the second or third day, ask a kind friend or partner with a gentle touch to give you a hand, foot or neck massage. Obviously steer clear of the site of the operation. The massage will help decrease post-operative 'blues' and promote physical relaxation. Use lavender oil, a natural relaxant.

Keep a bottle of lavender water to sprinkle on your pillow to aid rest and recuperation. In July or August, when lavender is in bloom, keep a little posy next to your bed; you will benefit from not only the aroma but the energy vibrations that the healing colour gives out.

Remedies

The purple dye extracted from *Murex* molluscs was used in ancient times to treat damaged tissue and draw pus from boils; it was believed that the special colour cured the complaint. In more recent times science has proved that the *Murex* mix formed calcium oxide, one of the compounds which was to lead to Dakin's antiseptic solution for the treatment of wounds, 2,000 years after its first use.

HEALING CRYSTALS AND GEMSTONES

- ***Amethyst*** – brings spiritual upliftment; helps in developing intuitive awareness; useful for increasing energy levels; eases stress; helps insomnia.
- ***Holley blue/purple*** – helps focus on your purpose in life; useful in channelling and healing work.
- ***Purple rainbow fluorspar*** – good for change; helps you get out of ruts.
- ***Rose quartz*** – promotes emotional balance and healing.

Healthy Colour Eating

Self-respect is reflected in the way you treat your body. As we saw earlier, purple is linked to the power to change, so to improve your self-esteem try some purple foods. As well as eating them and taking them into your body physically, you will also absorb their vibrations as they decorate your kitchen and as you prepare them.

Purple foods for thought include sumptuous shiny-skinned aubergines, plums, damsons, grapes and sensuous fresh figs. Try too purple sprouting broccoli and purple onions.

Using Purple to Make Changes

Purple, as already mentioned, is linked to the power to change damaging habits. If you tend to repeat your mistakes – like a photocopier that perpetually churns out a blotted image – purple will help you to let go of these behaviour patterns, as well as any feelings which are no longer relevant. If you are holding on to past hurts, past relationships which are no longer fulfilling, or any outworn thoughts and behaviour, this colour will help you move forward.

Purple is also a symbol of mourning; not the raw, tearing grief of black but a composed and dignified acceptance. This is the colour that can bring about dignified change. It is the hue of purpose, prayer and meditation.

Creative Visualizations with Purple

Dissolving negativity

mind

To release yourself from negativity, see yourself in a purple silk marquee, one of those huge tents that are hired for weddings. Imagine yourself fully covered and protected by beautiful purple rays. In the process see yourself letting go of all the fears and disappointments you have been holding on to. Let them float away through the sheer silk. Watch them dissolve into the scintillating blue sky. Affirm your ability to release all hindrances to your wellbeing.

Affirmations

- **I welcome positive joy into my life.**
- **My life is full of positive beginnings.**

The grace of spirit

This visualization is particularly beneficial for anyone struggling with the problems of addiction or compulsive attachment to damaging relationships.

Go to your safe space and quieten your breathing as you relax your body and prepare yourself (see pages 23–5).

Visualize the calm, ageless serenity of purple surrounding you. Perhaps you feel a swan's-down blanket being gently tucked around you. Feel the security of loving respect that covers you.

Pause.

With your next breath take in the purple air. Take it into your body and let it envelop your mind so that it fills every part of your being with the grace of spirit that dislodges old fears. As you breathe out, imagine you are expelling green, the complementary colour of purple. This green out-breath takes away any obsessions that have been with you and in their place leaves balance and harmony.

Pause.

As you rest in the dignity that is purple – the colour of completeness and the universal spirit – experience the wonder that is you. Marvel at the intricacy of your body and the wonderful work it does, every second of every day. Feel the blood flowing through your body carrying life-giving nourishment.

Respect your mind and the power it has to understand, create and communicate. Bathe your mind in the wisdom and self-respect of purple. Accept the true nature of your inner wisdom and let go of any self-doubt that has weakened you.

Pause.

See yourself as noble, as you truly are; no matter what your past, you did the best you could with the knowledge you had at the time. Whatever failures there were, now is the time to let them go. Release them as you continue your journey.

Let yourself travel to a mountain cave, the font of infinite wisdom. As you cross the threshold you see shafts of yellow, purple and orange light streaming through porthole shapes in the wall. In the lattice pattern of intermingled light you notice motes of gold gently drifting in the warm air that fills the roof space.

Pause.

Walk further inside so that the beams of light sparkle before you. Let the sense of eternity fill you. In this space, enveloped by purple majesty, you can let go of old habits and outworn beliefs. They served you in the past but now it is time to change, to take on the opportunity to live your life to the full. In the dignity of that purple and yellow mystical space, breathe in the acceptance that your life is precious.

Pause.

Look all around the interior. Is there any picture or sculpture which carries a message for you? Go closer and allow your eyes to focus on what is before you. Let it speak to the wisdom of your higher self which is always with you. In this quiet, respectful place it can be heard; through the silence it will speak to you. Perhaps it will not be in words, but in a sensation in your body, a warmth in your heart, or a blinding awareness that you can shed old, worn-out ways and embrace loving renewal.

Pause.

For a few more moments bathe in the glow of purple empowerment and then slowly make your way back to your safe space where you are now resting.

Imagine glowing white light gently creating a protective shield around you, preparing you to re-enter your everyday world.

Pause.

When you are ready, open your eyes.

Affirmations

- **Life gives me the opportunity to grow and learn.**
- **My spirit is bathed in healing grace.**
- **I can release old habits and embrace new healthy, loving relationships.**

Time to reflect

Make some notes about how you felt to use later in 'Sifting for Gold'.

Connection to the cosmos

First ensure you are relaxed in your comfortable safe space.

Imagine that you have a beautiful purple soft skullcap over the top of your head. Visualize that radiating from this skullcap are rays of brilliant light in various shades of purple. The rays travel down from the crown of your head so that they reach all of your body, from the top of your head to the tips of your toes.

Pause.

As you sit enveloped in these majestic rays you see a cloak of purple and violet. It soothes and kindles in you a powerful connection with the whole cosmos – a connection to every part of the universe so that each part is with you and a part of you. You feel you are part of this universal spirit. In that purple presence, you recognize your oneness with the whole world and experience a sense of your ultimate grace. You feel blessed and at the same time a part of the blessing.

Pause.

Allow your breath to travel smoothly from your solar plexus area right up to the crown. Breathe into your crown and feel an openness to higher inspiration.

Pause.

You feel the kindness of universal wisdom; you feel the purity that surrounds you and the lightness of being; you are at one with the universal spirit, the source of life and continuity. You are filled with a deep sense of inner peace and harmony. This purple light that courses through you and around you, heals your spirit. It heals the wounds that painful life experiences have inflicted on you. Whatever these wounds have been, however deeply you may have felt them, the spiritual intensity of the purple rays from your Crown Chakra can heal and make you new. The wisdom you have gained from these experiences will develop your sensitivity so that you become more caring to others whose path crosses yours.

You are at one with the universe and you are at peace. In the silence and the great calmness which surrounds you, absorb purple light into your body. You now feel expanded and complete. Allow the purple light gradually to be replaced with a pure white light.

The purple skullcap that has covered your crown now melts into the white light until the brilliant white light totally encircles you. You feel a connection to the whole universe still within you. The protective white light now allows you to come back into the space in which you are sitting.

Pause.

Feel the support of the chair or the floor on which you rest. Feel that connection and accept the beauty of your wisdom and knowledge, secure in the spiritual connection you have with the rest of the universe.

Affirmations

- **I am the universe, the universe is me.**
- **My life is a journey to spirit.**
- **My spirit is cherished and divine.**

Time to reflect

Write down the different sensations you felt during this visualization.

Creative Planting

When you use purple plants in visualizations, you allow your potential as a leader to flourish. As you breathe in the aromas of the flowers, the colour vibrations will surround you and bring the bloom of new awakenings to your spirit.

In *Colour By Design*, Sandra and Nori Pope show how you can control your garden palette by clever planting. Purple, because of its mixture of red and blue, is almost impossible to find in pure form, so look instead for shades of violet, plum and mauve.

PLANTING SUGGESTIONS – PURPLE, VIOLET, LILAC, MAGENTA

Spring	Crocuses, hyacinths, violets, cyclamens.
Summer	Lilac, foxgloves, stocks, delphiniums, *Nepeta* (catmint), *Buddleia davidii*, scabious.
Autumn	Asters, *Hebe* 'Autumn Glory'.
Winter	Purple-leaved sage, *Phormium* 'Purpureum', *Helleborus orientalis*.

VARIATIONS ON A THEME

Violet

Violet is the shortest wave in the physical spectrum and the colour of transformation. It acts as a depressant, slowing down active parts of the body except for the spine and the parathyroid. This colour will relax, calm and quieten the nerves of a person who is over-excited and allow the mind to be at rest.

Chakra Connection

Violet governs the Crown Chakra, which is linked to the pineal gland. This chakra is situated at the top of the head and covers the crown, the scalp and the brain. The pineal gland is sensitive to light and produces neurohormones that control all our bodily cycles, and so regulates our lives.

This violet chakra brings us to the wisdom of the universe and eternal truth. When you are open to this level of communication and take heed of what is offered, you can find a spiritual awareness that is denied to those who focus purely on more physical aspirations. Violet is the colour of the everlasting spiritual self which connects us to all that has been and will be.

The Crown Chakra holds the most evolved and developed energy within our human system and is, symbolically speaking, the highest aspect of the self. It is the centre of spiritual development, of beauty and emotional perception. It is home to the spiritual aspect of our human nature.

In ancient China, patients with the shaking sickness we now call epilepsy were placed on violet carpets in rooms with violet wall hangings and violet veils covering the windows. It was thought that being immersed in this calming colour reduced their anxiety and discomfort.

If you are the kind of person who finds it hard to love yourself, and are critical about almost everything you do and have a streak of punitive perfectionism, then violet visualization will help. Breathe in violet to increase self-respect and help you to accept the mantle of dignity that is your birthright. This is your true essence so let go of that damaging negativity.

Lilac

Lilac represents nostalgia and memories because it is made up of the pale-blue of loyalty and devotion and the pale-red of love. Lilac is the blossom of spring and the signal of new beginnings.

PAST MEMORIES

Lilac – rainbow, pastel, summer light, flowers, young and fresh, bright, bouncy, brilliance. Summer evenings, perfume, sunsets, sunny days on beaches . . . vibrant enthusiasm. Lilac represents all those things, perhaps as a reminder of things past that I have enjoyed.

Janet

Magenta

Magenta is sometimes associated with the eighth or spirit chakra, one of the three higher chakras accessed by the practice of profound meditation.

This is the colour of letting go of old emotions and habits in order to experience new physical and spiritual dimensions. If you want to make changes, relinquish worn-out ideas or patterns of behaviour, use magenta in your visualizations and include its complementary colour, green.

SHADES OF MAGENTA

Blank canvas with the colour creeping in from the sides, enveloping an Italian scene with tall houses and narrow streets. The sky colour creeping down from the top to the bottom. Shades of colour from pinky purple to dark purple – grapes, bottles of deep-plum wine. Swathes of silky material in all the shades of magenta hung like curtains, drawing back to reveal another layer and finally returning to the blank canvas. Then the whole process starts again . . .

P P

Now is the time to journey into the contrasting world of light and dark to discover the silver threaded into the deepest shadows.

7

The Shadows with Silver Linings

Darkness was at first by darkness hidden.

HINDU CREATION MYTH

Black and the Powers of Darkness

The Greek philosopher Plato gave us clues about the dark side of the way we think long before there were psychologists or psychiatrists. He likened the human mind to a chariot that was pulled by two horses, one black, one white. The white horse, the soul, was trying to climb to the heights of heaven, while the black horse, representing earthly, bodily desires, was attempting to plunge into the depths. The charioteer, our reasoning mind, the intellect, was trying to keep them both on track.

We can see that even then the idea that conflict, being pulled in all directions, was a part of being human. It is probably one of the reasons why black became synonymous with evil and was linked with sinking into depravity and the underworld. We inherited this legacy of negativity and echoes of it are still evident in our world today.

Another force of darkness, which is recorded in almost every culture under the sun, is the fear of what the night may conceal.

Black indicates an absence of light and typifies the powers of darkness, which are in direct conflict with the clarity of light. Black stands for defilement, mourning, error and annihilation. In 'Songs of Innocence' the poet and visionary William Blake describes black as being 'bereaved of light'. In Christian art black stands for penitence.

The 'black sun', twin of the solar sun, journeys through the dark once the daytime sun has set. People believed that it travelled to the blackest depths to rise again as the golden sun of daylight. This belief reflects the idea of duality, the yin/yang of life. The black sun came to signify the gods of the underworld. In astrology, Saturn, that most difficult of planets, is given black as its colour.

Black in Rituals

In the Vedic tradition of ancient India, black was associated with rain. To bring rain in a drought, the weather-doctor would put on black clothes edged in black frills in the form of feathers or ribbons. These signified black rain clouds and water droplets. He would also eat black food, symbolically incorporating the darkness of rain clouds into his own system, a kind of sympathetic magic: 'If I become as rain, I can control the rain and bring it to earth.' Other examples of this sympathetic magic can be seen in Native American dances where animal or bird costumes transmit their power to the wearer.

In parts of Africa an animal with a black coat – a sheep or a calf, for instance – would be sacrificed to make rain. As Fraser states in *The Golden Bough*: 'The colour of the animal is part of the charm; being black it will darken the sky with rain clouds.' Where drought can wipe out both livestock and whole communities, you can see the symbolic significance of black rituals.

The Black Dog of Depression

Medvedenko: Why do you wear black all the time?
Masha: I'm in mourning for my life, I'm unhappy.

Anton Chekov, *The Seagull*

Have you ever been hounded by 'the black dog'? Samuel Johnson was; he complained that it arrived at breakfast time and continued barking all day long. Winston Churchill was stalked by it too. 'The black dog' is the pet name for melancholia, or depression as it is called today. This link between the colour black and low spirits continues, but it may be linked to lack of light rather than unhappiness.

Seasonal Affective Disorder (SAD) causes people to feel varying degrees of depression during autumn and winter when there is reduced daylight. The symptoms include bouts of feeling down, low energy, increased need for sleep, carbohydrate craving and weight gain. SAD is more common in northern countries because the winter days are shorter so there is less energy-boosting light to fight the black moods. Recent research has found that light can be used to reduce the symptoms of

SAD. Phototherapy or exposure to bright, artificial light really can help. Just sitting under a lightbox for as little as half an hour a day can make significant improvements in 60–80 per cent of patients.

Black in Art Therapy

> **The mind is its own place, and in itself can make**
> **heaven of Hell, a hell of Heaven.**
>
> Milton

Many art therapists, as well as those who work with creative therapies where drawing and painting play an important role, find that people use black when depicting separation or loss. As Camilla Connell shows in her book *Something Understood*, which explores the significance of colour in art therapy with cancer patients, black holds a significant place.

Where black is mixed with red, we find a mixture of anger and depression, a warning to be careful. Sometimes black and red emphasize the dramatic intensity and conflict involved in personal trauma.

Turn out the Light, Turn on the Night

So far we have not captured the many glorious qualities of black, so we will look at those now.

From the cloak of darkness new life can spring, rising to the light. Crystals emerge from the pure darkness of the earth, from the energy centres of the earth and, as we have already discovered, have long been associated with healing. And how could the stars shine so brilliantly if it were not for the darkness of the night sky?

When we turn out the light we can enter the world of dreams. In dreams, dark shades conceal. Usually the dreamer associates this concealment with some form of threat. Negative combinations of colours are reflections of personal fears and reservations about aspects of our lives which disturb and challenge us. My book *Women Dreaming* gives many examples of how we can deal with such difficult, 'dark' dreams.

Black is Beautiful

Black can captivate the heart. Marc Chagall, the painter, poet and mystic, fell in love at first sight. Later he wrote of that first time he saw the beautiful Bella: 'Her pale face, her eyes. How big, round and black they are. They are my eyes, my soul. I knew that this was she – my wife.'

Black has always had a definitive part to play in cosmetics. Desmond Morris, in *Manwatching*, pointed out that the legendary beauty, Cleopatra, used black galena to define her eyebrows.

Mythical Connections

When Noah thought he might be nearing land, he first sent out a black dove. That was the beginning of the process which ended when the white dove returned with the olive branch.

Every year in ancient Greece, a ship sailed from Athens with black sails. This was the expiatory ship which symbolically carried away all the misdeeds and sins of the previous twelve months. It represented the atonement of Athenian citizens. When it returned from Crete and Delos it had white sails, the signal that the city could begin again with a clean sheet.

In ancient Rome the Law of the Goddess was engraved on black stone, lapis niger, thus forging a link between the female principle of creation and the colour black. The black stone built into the Kaaba at Mecca is a version of this and is still central to Muslim worship today.

Unlike most cultures, the Egyptians associated black with rebirth and resurrection so it was seen as essentially positive.

Black has traditionally been associated with the 'black arts', witchcraft and satanic practices. Witches, it was believed, could transform themselves into black cats, crows or black dogs. In the Salem witch trials that rocked America, the 'evidence' included statements that black familiars, as these creatures were called, had been roaming in the Puritan town. Unfortunately, the prejudice and hysteria cost many people their lives. Although now in different guises, much unwarranted prejudice against black still exists today.

Black sheep have traditionally been linked with bad luck. In Ireland, if the first lamb of the season was a black one it was said to foretell mourning for the family before the year was out. The black sheep of the family is the one who goes astray, falls onto hard times and generally brings disgrace to the family.

Overcoming Black Negativity

Stop thinking negatively about yourself. Stop giving yourself – and others – black looks! Positive self-talk helps; it promotes feelings of wellbeing because it influences our body chemistry by activating the parasympathetic nervous system, and enhances relaxation. If you are always putting yourself down, the purple visualization in the last chapter will help you to counteract the negativity of black. Purple, with its spiritual connections, will enable you to tune in to the highest aspect of yourself which empowers you to defeat feelings of self-loathing.

Creating dreaming space

Taking a nap or having a day-dreaming session for half an hour will really ease the strain if black gloom has been hounding you. Relax, then allow yourself to drift off for a sleep – it's well recommended: President Kennedy and Salvador Dali used to do it, and many other politicians and artists still do. Whether you sleep or daydream, it will give you the opportunity to wind down and recharge your batteries.

If half an hour seems far too indulgent, then give yourself ten-minute treats. Settle yourself comfortably, separate yourself from the worries of the world outside and let your mind explore these images of black. Explore too the counteracting influence of white and silver. When they are set against black, you can really appreciate their positive qualities; light becomes crystallized in a way that would not happen without the counteracting dark. Similarly, when you are in a gloomy depression and forced to face your vulnerability, others reveal their silver linings, their white purity of support.

Be kind to yourself

> **There are no mistakes, no coincidences.**
> **All events are blessings given to us to learn from.**
>
> Dr Elisabeth Kubler-Ross

If you can allow yourself to learn from whatever life puts in your path, you can reap the benefits. Elisabeth Kubler-Ross has spent her life working with the dying and transforming the attitudes of all those who come in contact with her. She teaches the importance of acceptance in both life and death and the recognition that we can all be healed.

Black and White Impressions

We were flying over America and suddenly I saw snow, the first snow we ever saw from orbit. I have never visited America, but I imagined that the arrival of autumn and winter is the same there as in other places, and the process of getting ready for them the same. And then it struck me that we are all children of our earth.

Aleksandra Aleksandrov, Russian cosmonaut

Looking at the stars always makes me dream, as simply as I dream over the black dots representing towns and villages on a map. Why, I ask myself, shouldn't the shining dots of the sky be as accessible as the black dots on the map of France?

Vincent Van Gogh

The surface of a slate-grey lake is lit
By the earthened lightning of a flock of swans,
Their feathers roughed and ruffling, white on white.

Seamus Heaney

Just now everything is still and white, snow, or the light on snow.

Janet Vuglar

Creative Visualizations to Dispel Blackness

Taking your dark side into the light

Relax and breathe calmly, following the technique on pages 23–5.

See yourself full of the brightest light you can imagine. Breathe in deeply. Feel all of your body filling with light.

Ask for a higher point of view, perhaps from someone who has expert knowledge about whatever it is that is bothering you, or from someone who has a vantage point giving a clearer, unhindered view into your world – or maybe from the complete wisdom of the universal spirit. And whatever that higher point of view is, accept that you *can* know the silver behind the dark. That illumination *is* available to you.

Ask for all the help you need to banish any feelings of darkness. Clear any fear out of your system, make room for more light, love and trust. Cleansing your system may involve loosening emotional ties. Are there any cords attached to you that hold you back? Any relationships which are cruel or hurtful or worn-out friendships maintained through habit rather than love?

Imagine that emotional cords from other people are attached to your chakras, then imagine those you no longer want being gently loosened and released. Watch them floating away; feel yourself getting lighter as other people's fears, demands and unrealistic expectations are separated out. Nothing can stay attached unless you want it to. Let harmful links be freed, for the benefit of yourself and others. The time is ripe for new beginnings.

Affirmations

- **My heart's desire for loving connection is fulfilled in every way.**
- **Happiness is assured, all fear is detached from me.**
- **I am at peace with myself and the world.**

Time to reflect

Make some notes to help you when you come to sift for gold in the final chapter.

VARIATIONS ON A THEME

Brown

Brown is the colour of mud, the substance of fertile ground where ideas and seeds are sown. On one of the oldest fertility statues ever found, the tiny Venus of Willendorf, there are traces of ochre colouring. The colour links it to the earth and the natural cycle of birth and death that is so visible in the landscape.

In Christianity, brown is sometimes linked to renunciation, which is why some religious orders such as the Franciscans wear this colour.

Creative Visualization with Brown

The dance of life

Steady your breathing. Relax and allow your body to find its own rhythm; just as in nature plants and animals find their rhythm in response to the sky, tides, weather and light. You are a part of this universe and respond to its inner signals, even though you may not be aware of it.

Once you feel free of tension, imagine a field of newly-turned, dark-brown soil. The rich earth is potent, ready to take seeds and nourish them. Imagine time passing. The cold and dark of winter comes on and it begins to snow. The cold climate frosts the landscape and purifies the earth. There is a sprinkling of snow – a blanket to cover the soil.

Pause.

The season moves on and in the spring sunshine, the earth looks lighter. An ochre sheen shows it is ready to take on the seed of life-giving plants. Wheat is planted in the light-brown soil, hidden from the light. In your mind you can see below the surface. You can see the tiny seed sending out shoots to secure nourishment from the giving earth. You can see a tendril seeking out the wonder of the life-giving sun. This is the law of nature; it has only to exist in its right place for growth to begin.

Below the soil you see the warmth of the spring sunshine and refreshing April rain quenching the thirst of the growing plant. The conditions are right for new life to emerge.

Pause.

You watch the first delicate green tips push their way through to the glory of a warm spring day. The world is ready for renewal and this is a sign to the world that the cycle of fertility is in place. The natural order is alive and well.

As you watch you see a celebration of the fertility of spring begin. In the moonlight, young men and women play instruments and dance around a tree, their circular movements echoing the eternal spinning of the sun and the planets. Their costumes of silver and green sparkle in the moonbeams. You feel one with this rite of spring that has taken place for millennia. Now, in your own way, celebrate the miracle of life. Feel the gift of life that is possible for all.

Let your vision turn inwards as the celebrants dance away to the valleys beyond, leaving the landscape empty of everyone except you, in your own life.

Pause.

Is there a need for enhanced fertility in you? Perhaps you want to be more creative in mind, body and spirit. You too have the potential to give birth to new life or new ideas. Perhaps you have been unsuccessful so far and this has made you sad and disappointed. If that is so, turn your attention to your own need and accept that below the surface of your outer life, at depths which are hidden from you, nature is at work.

Take a breath and breathe in the life-giving force of nature which longs to fulfil itself. You are part of that nature and have your place in the cycle of renewal. Breathe in the live-giving power of renewal and trust that in time you will be given outward signs that this process is happening. When the time is ripe you will know. Remember, ripeness is all.

Pause.

In the next breath, take the golden warmth of life into your heart. Let the silver of the moon, symbol of fertility, balance your life and grow within you. Then relax and feel yourself back in your special place, with your body in the room in which you are sitting or lying.

Affirmations

- **I celebrate my fertile creativity.**
- **I dance in the heart of light and life.**
- **The time is ripe for wonderful new directions in my life.**

Time to reflect
Record your thoughts and feelings to use later.

SOFT FUR BROWN

Warm, dark, colour of the earth, rich, soothing. Brown reminds me of autumn leaves and trees and walking through the woods in late sunshine. Brown eyes and chestnut hair; animals, soft fur. There are so many different shades: amber, hazel, auburn and ochre. This is such a nurturing colour, earthy and permanent. It's the colour of tanned skin, where warmth and sun have been captured inside it. It's oriental, exotic, and I just love it.

Titus

Silver

Black provides the perfect backdrop for a whole range of colours. A combination which is particularly dramatic and touches our universality is the silver of the moon and stars in a sea of infinite black. Silver is the metal associated with the moon.

Silver Linings

Starlight and moonlight are the sky's reflections of silver. In them we connect with the wider universe, with vistas beyond our everyday life on earth. Silver illuminates. By the light of the moon, dark paths are revealed.

The moon controls water and influences the tides. As we are mostly composed of water it is not surprising that it should influence us also. Certainly menstrual cycles are influenced by lunar cycles, as are our dreams, as I discovered when I was doing research for my book *Women Dreaming*.

The moon, always associated with silver, influences our moods too. Lunatics were so called because they were subject to the impact of the full moon, the lunar cycle. White witches wish on a piece of silver to reflect the moon and in Wicca, white magic, there are 13 moons all named after trees.

Silver has long been associated with protection and good luck. On the island of Skye off the coast of Scotland, a silver coin was often put under the threshold of a house when it was being built to ensure good fortune. A piece of silver on a necklace, string or chain was used in many countries as a charm against witchcraft. Silver is the bringer of good luck, and Mohammed forbade the use of any other metal in amulets except silver.

Silver has the power to pierce when other metals fail, and the legendary silver bullet was always sure to hit its target. There are many instances in history where the silver bullet was used successfully against a leader or mythical creatures such as vampires and bogles after other means had failed.

Reflections on Silver

Silver is associated with mirrors – as are reflection, illumination, and extending vision. Silver is the feminine quality and a fluid state. Like mercury (quicksilver), it is changeable and elusive: a quicksilver mind is one which allows its emotions to be spilt. They say a mirror never lies, as we see in the fairy story of Snow White when the evil stepmother asks 'Mirror Mirror on the wall, who is the fairest of them all?' The mirror reflects the truth.

A silver cord is supposed to connect the astral body to the physical body during dreaming and astral travel. When we die it is believed that this cord is severed and we move on to life on the other side.

To ensure calmness where there has been upset, introduce silver into your wardrobe or home with silver earrings, silver jewellery, accessories with silver threads in, or silver objects such as candlesticks and frames.

In the same way that there is light after darkness, there is silver in the shadows. In the diamond glints of this poem, whose origins remain a mystery, there is unending life.

Do not stand at my grave and weep;
I am not there. I do not sleep.
I am a thousand winds that blow.
I am the diamond glints on snow.
I am the sunlight on ripened grain.
I am the gentle autumn rain.
When you awaken in the morning's hush
I am the swift uplifting rush
Of quiet birds in circled flight.
I am the soft stars that shine at night.
Do not stand at my grave and cry;
I am not there. I did not die.

Unknown

Renewal and regeneration are indivisible from life and living.

8

Tones of Tranquillity

Be of little substance and become the Light.

LARRY MOEN

As we have already seen, colour has a powerful impact on personality and behaviour. Turning to calming, soothing tones we find that there are particular colours or tonal ranges to quieten. When grey is added to a colour it is called a tone, when white is added it is called a tint.

White

White symbolizes light, triumph, purity and innocence. It is the emblem of supreme, divine power, probably because of the intense whiteness of the sun and its triumph over darkness.

Mythical Connections

The sacred horses of Greek, Roman, Germanic and Celtic cultures were all white. The knight on a white horse symbolizes the hero rescuer who represents pure love and courage triumphing over dark forces.

On the first day of the new year the Roman consul would dress in white robes and ride up to the Capitol on a white horse to celebrate the triumph of Jupiter, the god of light, over the spirit of darkness. Romans marked auspicious, lucky days with white chalk and inauspicious days with charcoal. In heraldry, white or silver, known as 'argent', represents faith and purity.

White Light

Isaac Newton (1642–1727), the father of modern physics, found that white light was in fact much more complex than people believed. He discovered that when white light was refracted through a prism, it separated to become a wondrous mixture of rays. He chose to describe seven hues – red, orange, yellow, green, blue, indigo and violet – and linked them to the seven planets, as well as to notes on the musical, diatonic scale. The rainbow from white light was an amazing discovery at the time.

Tones and Tints

Light tones look soft and comforting, like fleecy clouds. Pale pastels soothe the spirits because they are peaceful, quiet and less stimulating than other more raucous colours in the spectrum. Grey is a neutral, borderline colour, and can feel non-committal.

Let your mind focus on these colours from nature. Spend a minute on each one and note how you feel, and any different sensations you experience.

- soft mauves, lilac and lavender
- pale peppermint greens
- dusky, yellowy oranges
- mustard buttercups
- the washed-out lemon of primroses
- beech and light oak
- apricots and creamy peaches
- soft tones of terracotta
- oatmeal and calico
- coral

Very often these colours induce feelings of nurturing warmth. They feel safe and serene, causing us to experience a sense of wellbeing which is particularly helpful when stress abounds. Soft warm colours speed healing and help us feel calmer.

Use these short colour visualizations to centre yourself and to recapture the feeling of being a cherished part of the universe.

Creative Visualizations with Quiet Colours

Tranquil times

Go through your relaxation routine (pages 23–5).

Focus on the slow, deep breaths coming from your diaphragm. See and feel the breath coming in through your solar plexus rather than your mouth. Once you are comfortable with that feeling, feel the breath turn into brilliant white light, which enters through the stomach and flows everywhere in your body, bringing with it healing and free-flowing energy. Do this for as long as you would like, keeping the breath slow, deep and regular.

Pause.

If there is a particular part of the body that you would like to work on, shift your attention there. Feel the light entering as though you were breathing it in. For example, imagine your breath is coming in through the top of your head or through your heart. Continue to breathe in white light and then let it change to tints of yellow, soft gentle shades of harmonious tranquillity.

Visualize looking at yourself in a mirror. See every aspect of your body clearly – not as you are, but as you would like to be. For example, if you are trying to heal a scar on your hand, see your hand clearly with healthy skin and no scar. Stare at it, seek every detail. If you are trying to lose a certain amount of weight, see yourself as you would look after that weight has gone. Be specific.

If you are ill, see and feel yourself totally well and vibrantly healthy. See yourself doing things in great detail in a healthy body. See yourself as you were at a point in your life when you felt in peak condition. See your hair shining, your eyes sparkling.

See yourself surrounded by gentle tones that are soothing and peace-giving and, as you take your attention back to the room, keep that sense of tranquillity with you.

Affirmations

- **I see myself in perfect, shining health.**
- **I have a perfect ability to make myself radiant in mind, body and spirit.**
- **My spirit is soothed by the tranquillity of nature's grace.**

Time to reflect

Make any notes you need to help you when you turn to Chapter 10, 'Sifting for Gold'.

Bathing bonus

Go through the relaxation process and, when you are ready, try this personal visualization.

Think of your favourite colour. Now, imagine yourself wrapped in this colour. Feel yourself enveloped in it, resting in its hues; feel it drenching your pores. Drink in the colour and see what tastes it evokes. Does it make you think of particular foods or fruits?

After you are fully satisfied by your colour bath, imagine white being added to your chosen colour. See how it slowly mixes in, softening and reducing the first colour's intensity. At any point where you feel enough has been added, you can stop.

How does this new tint feel? Does it bring out a softer, gentler side of your nature? Give yourself the space to explore what your life would be like if you expressed this aspect of yourself. How would others react to you?

Often a harsh exterior masks betrayed hopes, but hopes can live again, trust can be restored. As you bring your visualization to a close, enjoy the comforting, kind warmth of your new colour. Celebrate the calming effect of white.

Affirmations

- **Gentleness brings joy to my life.**
- **Whatever has gone before, now I am renewed and am the loving person I am meant to be.**
- **Whatever I do for others, I do for myself.**

A mystery gift

Use the relaxation process to prepare you for a special empowerment visualization, one with a more practical aspect this time.

Choose a tranquil colour. Feel yourself bathing in the glory of this colour. See it showering down on you, pouring through your hair and over your shoulders, hugging your body right the way down to the soles of your feet. Feel it hovering near you as you dry off.

Then, as you rest suffused in the colour you have chosen, perhaps with the addition of a flash of yellow for learning and wisdom, you see an object. This is for you. It might be large or small, a square shape like a box, or an irregular shape like a machine. Make it any shape you wish but ensure it is wrapped in the colour of your choice and know that it requires active involvement from you.

Whatever it is, it comes with a set of instructions. Don't worry about the object you have chosen – honour your inner wisdom and accept the first thing that comes to mind. You can leave it behind later if you want to.

What is in your package? Is it something from the past? Something you've always wanted? What do you feel about it? What do the instructions say? Are they easy to follow or garbled and unclear? Do they help you understand the machine or object that was given to you? Think about your response to this new information; it can reveal a lot about the way in which you prefer to learn.

Visualization gives you the power to choose how you want life to be, so if you found yourself frustrated by these instructions, make yourself some better ones.

The way you approach new tasks is helped or hindered by your previous experience, your level of confidence and your openness to learning. Try these affirmations if you want to change your approach.

Affirmations

- **I am open to new learning.**
- **My calmness is my key to success.**
- **Quiet reflection helps me work things out.**

Personal experience

When Liam did the 'mystery gift' visualization he found that he had been given a flat-pack chest, the sort you can use as a coffee table. He was pleased with the 'gift' but quickly got annoyed with the instructions. First, there was a whole sheaf of loose papers; secondly, there were about ten different languages to wade through; and thirdly, the writing was so small he wondered if he needed glasses! What was this about?

When we talked he explained that being calm was difficult for him and his reaction in the visualization was typical. Instead of approaching tasks slowly and methodically, he quickly gets irritated and makes matters worse. (In the visualization he threw the instructions on the floor and the sheaf of papers scattered everywhere – they were not numbered!)

To gain from the insight of this visualization, Liam and I worked together to create the most perfect set of instructions he could wish for: specific language, easy-to-follow bullet points and large print. He realized that he could give himself an easier time if he did not keep repeating old failure patterns.

Tranquil Home and Hearth

In her book *Spirit of the Home*, Jane Alexander tells the story of Hestia, goddess of the hearth. Hestia, also known as Vesta, is the centre of the home, the hearth, the heart of warmth and wellbeing. The round central hearth in every home was symbolically and literally the focus of life, where people would gather and keep warm and cook. The circle is the symbol of the earth and in prehistoric excavations the fires were always circular in the centre of the dwelling place. Today, whilst you may not have a live fire in your home, you can use a lighted candle to symbolize the importance of this meeting point between earth and sky. The earth grounds you whilst the fire or candle flame reaches to the heavens. Hestia was the spirit of the home, providing calm and an opportunity for quiet reflection and order.

Your home is a statement about who you are and how you see yourself. Take an imaginary physical journey around your home right now. Let your eyes linger and your senses investigate. Is it fresh and clean? Is it decorated in colours that reflect who you are? Does the space provide you with restful calm where you need it?

Clutter represents stagnant energy and holding on to the past for fear that the future will not provide you with what you need. If you have no space for the new, how can you expect your life to change?

Come home to the place in your heart where you feel natural and at peace and at one with yourself and your environment. Choose your own pattern rather than clinging onto other people's. You are leading your own life; it is not up to somebody else to direct it for you.

Creative Visualization with Hestia, Goddess of the Hearth

Your perfect home

Start by going through your tried and tested relaxation technique.

Visualize yourself walking up to the door of your perfect home. What colour is the door? Really look carefully at this entrance way and when you are ready walk in.

Pause.

In ancient Greece and Rome the hallway was considered to be the transition point between the outer and inner world, between the domain of Hermes, god of worldly matters, and Hestia, goddess of the hearth. Take time to pause on the threshold and let yourself become centred, ready to leave the outside demands to focus on this, the heart and centre of your home.

Pause.

Think of the sounds you want in your home. See yourself sitting down at a table for breakfast, what do you hear? Is it birdsong, the babbling of a stream outside your window? Perhaps it's the noise of boats on a river or bicycle bells on a cycle route. Whatever you want to hear you can have.

What about the other sounds in your home? Are there other people's voices, children laughing perhaps, or the purr of a cat? As you allow the sounds of your ideal home to come to you, feel free to choose whatever your heart desires. Is it in the country or a city? Quiet or bustling? Choose whatever feels right for you; there are no right answers, only personal preferences.

Imagine you are sitting in the most comfortable armchair and listening to your choice of music. What music can you hear?

Pause.

Imagine you are walking from room to room. As you go through your perfect home be aware of the scents that reach you. Aromas can be either welcoming and comforting or harsh and antiseptic. What smells make you feel comfortable? The smell of fresh laundry that has dried in the open air? The pine smell of newly-mopped floors? The scent of lavender oil from an aromatherapy burner? Imagine the smells of each room wafting to you as you tour your perfect home.

Pause.

In your perfect home imagine the textures and feel of the fabrics around you. What would give you the utmost pleasure? Cool linens, silky sheets, velvet curtains? What about floor coverings? See yourself walking from bathroom to bedroom to sitting area. Are the textures beneath your bare feet different in each space? Be aware of the sensuous pleasure of these different textures against your skin.

Pause.

As you dream up your perfect home space, remember it does not need to be vast and expensive. But what it does need is loving thought. Your senses will flourish and your creativity blossom as you learn what would truly make your home your heart space.

Visualize your ideal home in the perfect setting for you. You may feel that where you live is exactly what you want; if so celebrate that. If not, then give yourself time to put all your images of colours, textures, aromas and tastes together and allow yourself to truly know this place that is waiting for you. As you visualize it, so you set in train a process that can make it happen. Allow yourself to dream and you open yourself to positive changes in your life.

Pause.

Soon you will be leaving your perfect home. Before you return, ask Hestia, the goddess of the hearth, to give you a blessing. What would you ask her to give your home? Let your heart ask for what would make your space a centre of spiritual nourishment.

Pause.

Now take your attention back to the room in which you sit. Feel the surface of the space where you are sitting or lying down.

Affirmations

- **My home is my happiest haven.**
- **Loving energy fills me whenever I sit in the heart of my home.**
- **The music of universal harmony sings in my soul.**

Time to reflect
Make some notes confirming the qualities you think would make your living space more appealing.

We leave tranquil tones behind now to explore the brilliance and variety of the seven colours of the rainbow.

9

The Rainbow of Radiance

The simple blessing of a rainbow . . .

DANNY ABSE

Rainbows contain all the colours of the spectrum. Throughout the ages they have captured the imagination of mankind with their purity and brilliance. In addition, because these arcs of colour touch both the earth and the sky, they have been invested with a mythical and mystical power, which is present with us still.

How are Rainbows Formed?

Water molecules in the air act like millions of tiny prisms. As the sun's rays fall on the almost spherical droplets of water, they are reflected and refracted so they appear as coloured rays. These then arrange themselves into the bands of colour that make up the arc in the sky. A rainbow is the most dramatic example of white light being broken up.

Chakra Connection

Colour therapists believe that our body is a crystal which takes in the white light of the sun and reflects the seven colours of the rainbow back to the universe via the chakras.

The pituitary gland, the master endocrine gland at the base of the brain, is the inner prism that breaks down the light (energy) and distributes it to the body through the chakras. The rainbow in our body is really the colour coding of the chakras which echo the endocrine system. To refresh your memory, red is the energy centre at the base of the spine, orange is just below your navel, yellow is the solar plexus area, green is the heart place, blue is the throat, indigo is the middle of the forehead and violet is the crown of your head. And white light is the perfect blending of all the colours which protect and heal us, as we have discovered in earlier chapters.

Rainbow Myths

Symbolically, rainbows have always had a unique place in every cultural tradition. One of the best-known in the West is the story of the rainbow that appeared to Noah after the flood. God spoke to Noah and said, 'I do set my bow in the cloud and it shall be for a token of a covenant between me and the earth.' (Genesis). With this covenant God promised Noah that He would never again send a flood to destroy the world and His sign was always to be the rainbow. Thus it is now firmly established as a symbol of hope and a bridge between heaven and earth.

In a Babylonian myth which predates the Noah story, the goddess Ishtar is said to have placed a rainbow in heaven in order to block the god who had caused a devastating flood. Later Ishtar wore a rainbow around her neck, though this is often translated as seven different-coloured veils. Although the legendary dance of the seven veils of her priestess Salome now has a place in the history of eroticism, and seven remains a number associated with magic or mystery.

Traditionally, the rainbow is regarded as the celestial bridge over which gods may walk whilst men go beneath – a link between the unseen world of the spirit and the seen material world of everyday life. In Australia, however, the rainbow is associated with the Divine Snake, one of the most powerful creative forces in the universe. In Aboriginal culture, the Rainbow Serpent is as vital to an understanding of creation as Adam and Eve are to a Christian culture or the 'Big Bang' to an atheistic, scientific one. The Aborigines of Arnhem Land believe the Rainbow Serpent Mother made the world and gave birth to all people in all their varying shades. Like the rainbow, the Serpent symbolizes the interconnection of all colours and all mankind.

Build Yourself a Rainbow

Think for a moment about rainbows you have seen: in bubbles, in puddles on the road or on wet window panes. Allow yourself the pleasure of focusing on their wonderful hues and let yourself delight in the joy they bring. Can you recall seeing a rainbow as a child? Can you recapture the surge of happiness that flashed through your body? Cherish that connection with delight and breathe in the rainbow.

Next time you go shopping why not buy yourself a multi-faceted crystal to hang as a rainbow catcher in your window. As the light shines through the crystal, rainbows will beam into your room. Try different sizes hung in different places to maximize the effect.

Healing with Rainbows

The Ancient Egyptians used rainbow colours in their hieroglyphics, as shown in a veritable rainbow of cures written on a papyrus scroll dating from 1550 BC. It includes the use of red lead, black lizards and verdigris, the beautiful green copper salt. Theo Gimbel, in his *Colour Therapy*, explains how the Egyptians mixed verdigris with beetle wax as a treatment for cataracts.

In Egyptian healing temples the sun shone through expertly placed gems, rubies and sapphires on to the person seeking healing. In the brilliant rainbow all kinds of ailments from stomach disorders to infertility were treated. And, as a final rainbow potion, gemstones were crushed to be eaten or drunk.

A lovely healing visualization is described by Lilian Verner-Bonds in *Colour Healing*. She suggests you visualize a beautiful rainbow all around your body, as if you were inside a circle like an egg yolk. Next you imagine the seven colour bands of the rainbow floating around you. You then let your body absorb the colours it needs. Whatever colour you need, she says, your inner light will bring it to you.

Crossing the Bridge

Rainbows are symbolically linked to death for they symbolize the transition – the bridge – from physical life to the life of the spirit in another dimension. In many drawings done by both children and adults nearing their time of death, images of rainbows spontaneously appear, even if they have not known that death was imminent. Similarly, in dreams rainbows give solace and a wondrous sense of safe transition from one part of life to another.

In his book *Who Dies?*, Stephen Levine, international author and consultant on death, dying and meditation, revealed how rainbow meditations were crucially important in preparation for death:

> **Unlike our culture which encourages little preparation for death, in the American Indian culture at the time of death a naturally formed**

crystal is often offered for use as a meditation object. Gazing into the fissures within the crystal that create prismatic rainbow lines, one projects one's consciousness into the rainbow, letting go of all that keeps the mind from focusing beyond itself. At death one is guided into the rainbow body, melting out of temporal form with ease and wise preparation.

Finding a Positive Path

When you are trapped in a damaging rut or feel emotionally stuck, it is very hard to set yourself free. Though you know you are being physically depleted and feel psychologically drained, often you cannot summon up the energy to escape your various health problems. As you sink deeper into this negative rut, you may well become more prone to physical or psychological illness. The following visualizations will help you drive out those old self-defeating habits.

Creative Visualizations with Rainbow Colours

Opening up to the universal life force

To open up the channel of communication within your body, picture a column of white, purifying light. Let yourself be surrounded by it. Next see the white light change as rainbow colours pour from it.

Breathe in this rainbow through your nose, taking it down into your body so that the radiating energy can bring you new zest. The rainbow, sign of hope, bringer of wonder to every place it touches, no matter how poor or damaged, is a piece of magic that illuminates our world. Breathe it in to give you inspiration. Allow the universal life force to flow through every cell in your body.

Absorbing rainbow energy

Visualize yourself surrounded by pure white light. With your inner vision see yourself bathed in this wonderful glow. It protects you and gives you insight into the full range of possibilities that life presents to you.

Visualize the Crown Chakra begin to open as though it were a flower opening to the first rays of the sun. Let all the rays of rainbow energy flow one by one down through your crown. Let it be your prism which transforms white light. Pause after each colour.

First bring in the warmth of red and let it travel through your body. Imagine it bringing warmth and energy to every part of you. As it travels from your head down to your feet, imagine it flowing out of your toes to energize the world around you.

Next let the energy of orange flow from your head to your toes, bringing renewed vitality to each cell of your body. Let it flow through you to re-energize the earth.

The bright wisdom of yellow is next. Let its radiance fill your head as if the sun were blessing you with glowing health. Feel the wisdom of yellow saturate each part of you as it flows down your arms and body until it rolls into the ground, warming roots and seeds on its journey to the earth's heart.

Then let cool calming green, the balancing colour, rinse through your body. Feel it easing all tensions as it harmonizes mind, body and spirit. Let it flow through you until it washes down into the earth to connect once more with the natural greens of the meadow grass.

The cleansing purity of blue now spreads through your body. Visualize it shining on the crown of your head then feel each atom of your being suffused with blue. Let it clear away unwanted thoughts and fears; let it cleanse and heal you. As the tide of blue flows out, let it wash into the seas of the planet.

Next let indigo and violet ripple through every vein and artery; let them lift your spirit and increase your willingness to experience new hope and awareness. Once these colours have expanded into the wholeness that is you, allow them to dissolve out through every pore to heal the hurts of our planet.

Finally, surround yourself once more with the perfect blend of white light.

Affirmations

- **I am filled with the rainbow of radiance.**
- **Every colour reflects my brilliance.**

Blue remembered hills

This visualization features all the colours of the spectrum so that you can fully appreciate how they work together. Think of the colours as actors in a play, each with a personal role, or in this case a particular vibration and power. When actors come together and form a cast, the story unfolds from their different perspectives. Similarly, when you work with all the colours in the spectrum you include all their strengths. The blending of their individual qualities leads to a greater intensity, depth and range of expression.

Settle into your special visualization place and allow your breathing to become calm and relaxed.

Visualize a favourite place in the countryside, a place where you feel relaxed and safe. If you cannot recall a place then imagine a place you would like to be in. When you have done this, enjoy the beauty of your surroundings.

You are now going to travel further from your chosen spot, towards the horizon. As you look into the distance you see a range of mountains. Distant hills look uniformly blue – blue-remembered hills which are steeped in history.

As you look towards them you can see through veils of shimmering colour a landscape that has supported the richest of lives. You see sparkling mountain streams splashing through crystal rocks, bringing pure water for all to drink. Still pools reflect the azure sky and wild strawberries, rich red, tumble over the edges.

Pause.

You find that your favoured spot has changed to include some of the wonder of those distant hills. Go towards the sparkling stream, taste the freshness of the mountain air, see the light glinting on the wet rocks. Pick an exquisite berry, feel the tender juice on your tongue, experience the vibrancy it brings to you as you take in the health-giving red energy. Subtle and gentle energy rippling through your body.

Pause.

The mountains echo with the sound of centuries of people carrying gifts and health-giving berries.

The brilliant white sun has dipped in the sky now. There at the mountain's crest you see its full red emblazoning the sky with glorious rays. Those rays reach to you, surrounding you and wrapping you in 'wondrous light'. A rainbow of light pulses through your body.

Pause.

Your heart affirms the beauty of your being. Say these affirmations to yourself to seal the power of the visualization.

Affirmations

- **I allow my light to shine from within.**
- **My place in the world is a place of wonder and delight.**
- **I am wrapped in rainbows of creativity.**

Picture the scene

This visualization takes a different form from the others you have done so far, but it is just as powerful and extends your repertoire of visualization techniques. You will need a piece of A4 paper, some coloured pencils, crayons or felt-tipped pens, and at least 15 minutes of uninterrupted time.

You are going to draw an outdoor scene. It can be in any kind of landscape, with or without people, with or without animals or birds; in other words, put down whatever comes to mind, however wild or fanciful. It is your scene so you can do exactly what you like. This is not about artistic ability; rather, it is about letting your inner voice sing and letting your inner vision work for you. Take your time and enjoy the process. When you allow yourself to draw and really get into it, you activate the same part of the brain as meditation does, so you will gain alpha wave calmness and clarity as well as your completed picture.

When you have finished, give your scene a title and use the points and questions below in readiness for sifting for gold in Chapter 10.

Time for reflection

What are the main colours in the drawing? Are you present? If so, what are you doing? Who else is there? What are they doing?

What is the shade of the sky or background – for example, is it dark, bright or dull? Count any particular groups or sets – people, animals, flowers, grasses, trees, etc, and write them down.

Is there anything in your picture that surprises you? If so, what and why?

Add any other comments you think are relevant. Keep your picture safe. We will return to its message in the next chapter.

Colour poem

I am the green bud growing, the gold in ripened barley.
I am the pink of dawn, the red of raspberry lips.
I am the black of polished coal, the white of diamond snow.
I am the indigo of the night sky, and the blue of eternity.
Let my colours rainbow the earth and be the bridge
between worlds.

We leave the rainbow behind now to seek for nuggets of pure gold.

10

Sifting for Gold

The sun with all the planets revolving around it, and depending on it, can still ripen a bunch of grapes as though it had nothing else in the universe to do.

GALILEO GALILEI

When I was choosing a title for this chapter, at first I could not decide between 'Dredging for Gold', 'Going for Gold' or 'Sifting for Gold'. 'Dredging', though it fitted the idea of going below the surface, felt too heavy and sluggish. 'Going for Gold' felt too Olympian and driven somehow, so I settled for 'sifting'. It encompasses what I hope will happen for you here when you look back at the many visualizations, writing and drawings you have done. It is a gentle, reflective approach which gives you time to sort out what is important to you. This is the section in which you sift for gold, searching out nuggets of wisdom from all the visualizations you have done whilst working through the book. You will gain valuable insights into your strengths, creativity and inner wisdom as you sieve through your collection of notes and process all the information that is to be found there. All your efforts will be rewarded when you discover just how much there is to learn about your deeper self.

Nuggets of Gold

First of all, let us look at the qualities of gold. Ultimately, the power of gold comes from its identification with the sun because, like the sun, it is 'immortal', unceasing. It never fades and is indestructible. It is bright shining wisdom, glory and glorious revelation. It is the colour of the champion, the Olympic winner, the 'golden boy'. Gold is the colour of Easter, when eggs are wrapped in glittering gold foil to celebrate the renewal of life after death.

You often see gold used in marketing to promote the idea of excellence. In the world of plastic cards, the gold one gets virtually unlimited credit; in health clubs, gold cards are the ones which allow access at all times to all facilities; and golden globes signify the highest achievements in the world of drama. Golden weddings tell us of vows unbroken and an unending connection. Silence too is golden, especially when it lets you hear your inner voice, a priceless connection.

Gold Currency

Gold is what you take when there is no other currency to see you through. It is the passport for refugees who flee terror, because on the black market and in times of war, gold is the only exchange that is accepted. It is the colour of abundance, treasure, and Spanish doubloons. A golden halo shows that a saint has achieved spiritual maturity and moved beyond earthly hurts to connection with the ultimate spirit. Golden light rays symbolize spiritual radiance. Those emitted by Christian saints, or portrayed symbolically in the elaborate golden headdresses of Egyptian Pharaohs, represent auras. They are seen in icons, churches and temples.

Gold is associated with wisdom and is the symbol of transmutation, a process by which alchemists changed base metals – iron for instance – into precious gold. As Barbara G Walker points out in *A Woman's Dictionary of Symbols and Sacred Objects*, the alchemical sign for gold is the same as the symbol of the sun. Fire can melt gold but it is an 'immortal' metal and will not be destroyed. It is also linked to the search for the Holy Grail, the golden chalice, which symbolizes the attainment of true grace after enormous struggle.

How do you think these qualities are linked to your life quest? What can you learn from your journey so far?

Mythical Connections

Sun worship is as old as the human race and there are legends in many different cultures which explain the origins of this all-powerful, life- and light-giving sun. The Egyptian god Ra, it was believed, once lived on earth but was driven out by man's wrongdoing. He fled to the upper skies and his eye became the sun. The sun symbolized his masculine strength and greatness.

Across the world in cold Britain, where the rays of the sun were less in evidence, the Druids built temples to the sun. And the image of the sun god was printed on gold coins by the first Christian emperor, Constantine I, and inscribed 'the invincible sun, my guardian'.

Golden mystical animals are found in many legends: the golden goose which laid the golden egg promising never-ending fortune; the golden cow which was worshipped in ancient Egypt as a symbol of the god Horus, worshippers placed gold on altars dedicated to this son of Isis. And the search for the Golden Fleece was Jason's arduous task.

Worth more than gold?

King Midas, whose touch turned everything to gold, soon learnt that human contact was more valuable than a metallic world devoid of pulsing, growing life, no matter how much money it was worth.

Native Americans did not see gold in terms of wealth. As Marie Herbert says in *Healing Quest*, they thought of gold as the excrement or sweat of the sun. Sculpting it into an article of beauty was considered a way of honouring this spiritual force, and wearing it an act of humility.

Gold amulets were placed in the coffins of Egyptian Pharaohs to give health and protection in the world to come. And Bavarian farmers would wear a gold ring as they sowed their grain to ensure it ripened to a rich colour.

As the saying goes 'All that glisters is not gold' and 'fool's gold' – iron pyrites of a grassy yellow colour – has no substance or financial value. The pot of gold at the end of the rainbow is the treasure we all desire, like the winning lottery ticket, but its elusiveness might well be our salvation, so beware of false promises and the fake shine of fool's gold.

Healing with Gold

Gold injections are given in cases of severe rheumatoid arthritis. Gold lifts depression by putting a glow of wellbeing on the sufferer and is also good for healing past hurts.

In 1387 Chaucer recorded in the *Canterbury Tales*, the power of gold to cure. Wedding rings were rubbed on sore eyes, for instance, if someone had a sty or 'red eyes', which we now know as conjunctivitis. Sailors, it is said, had their ears pierced with a gold ring to strengthen their sight, and in Norfolk in the UK, fishermen believed that by wearing gold earrings they would be immune from drowning (in fact, sailors have been wearing earrings since the time of Elizabeth I).

The healing properties of gold were known to the ancient Egyptians, Greeks and Chinese, and to the wise healers of Tibet, Persia and India. Similarly, both the Mayans of South America and Native Americans knew the power of light made visible that gold represented; however, when the Dark Ages swept across the West, the light was snuffed out. Now at this time it is being rekindled. How can you use gold in your life now?

Gold and silver rays

In some colour therapies gold rays are used for balancing masculine energy in a person, because gold embodies the masculine aspect. Silver rays are used for balancing feminine energy, because silver embodies the feminine aspect. When the sun and moon, gold and silver, are in balance, then all is right with the world.

You can achieve this balance by wearing either gold or silver jewellery, depending on which is needed; you can also apply this technique in creative colour. In your meditations or as you are relaxing, visualize gold rays coming from your Crown Chakra and silver rays travelling up from your feet, or simply imagine being showered with alternate rays of gold and silver.

Creative Planting

Enjoy the time to breathe in these yellow and gold vibrations.

PLANTING SUGGESTIONS – SPLASHES OF GOLD

Spring	Crocuses, daffodils, laburnum.
Summer	Yellow lilies and amaryllis, sunflowers, black-eyed Susan.
Autumn	Cape dandelions, golden rod, yellow gentians, *Rudbeckia*.
Winter	Variegated ivy, winter jasmine.

A Golden Gift

Imagination is more important than knowledge.

Albert Einstein

When prospectors panned for gold in the heady days of the gold rush, they sieved through their collected stones to find the purest pieces of gold which would guarantee wealth. In this part you will sieve through visualizations in order to discover symbolic gold nuggets which can enrich you physically, mentally and spiritually.

'To a New Shore' Revisited

In this visualization (see page 75) you received a gift. Now is the time to explore the meaning of this gift in more depth. Write the word for your gift in the middle of a piece of paper. Then note any words you associate with it. Be as free as you can and don't let your 'spoilsport censor' stop you writing whatever comes into your head. This is for you, don't worry about whatever anyone else might think. Then look through your collection of words and see what connections you can make.

The diagram on page 129 shows what I wrote down following a visualization where my gift was an oyster – quite a shock, but it's important to accept whatever presents itself! I was surprised at this gift because I have only ever tried to eat oysters once and I thought they were awful, but prior to this tasting, I had once collected them when on holiday with my family in France.

I explored my response by dividing the words into a variety of categories (see page 130).

Exploring the results

I was surprised at how many images of strength came out in the qualities list, and at the contrasts between the openness and closedness of the image: open it is beautiful, rare and elemental; closed it is deep, hard to kill, clinging and strong. How much does this reflect the open directness of my personality and the deeper, more concealed vulnerable side of myself? By exploring these aspects I learnt a great deal about myself at that point in my life.

You may also find it helpful to do a drawing or a painting of the object you chose. Then spend time exploring your image and see what comes to light.

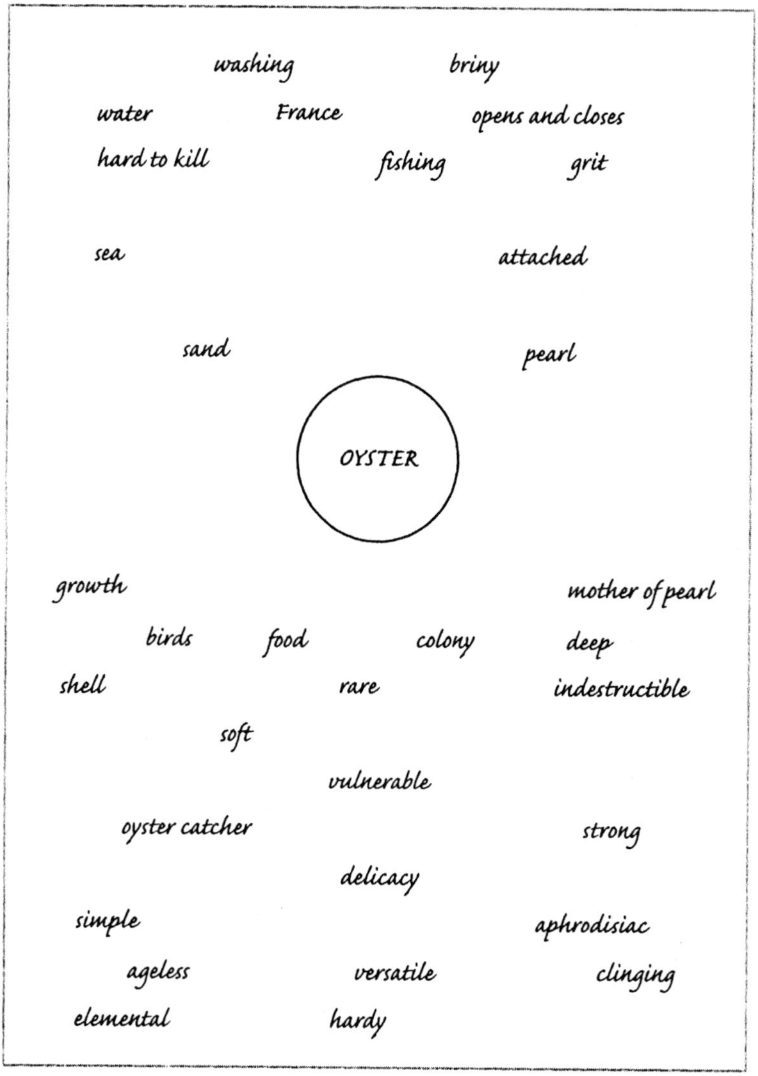
washing
briny
water
France
opens and closes
hard to kill
fishing
grit
sea
attached
sand
pearl
OYSTER
growth
mother of pearl
birds
food
colony
deep
shell
rare
indestructible
soft
vulnerable
oyster catcher
strong
delicacy
simple
aphrodisiac
ageless
versatile
clinging
elemental
hardy

Qualities	*Places*	*Of the Spirit*
hard to kill	France	ageless
attached	deep	elemental
indestructible	sea	
aphrodisiac	sand	
clinging	water	
ageless	colony	
versatile		
hardy		
elemental		
simple		
soft		
strong		
briny		

Activities	*Nourishing*	*Precious*
growth	food	pearl
washing		mother of pearl
clinging		rare
opens and closes		birds
fishing		oyster catchers

What Your Paintings Reveal

Spontaneous drawings and paintings can reveal so much because they speak straight from the creative heart rather than being processed through the logical side of your brain. This means they often hold surprising nuggets of previously unrealized truths about our desires, fears and potentials. They are also very good problem solvers, so see what you can find as you sift for gold.

Colours as clues

> **Colour and I are one. I am a painter. Colour has taken hold of me; no longer do I chase after it. I know that it has a hold of me forever. That is the significance of this blessed moment.**
>
> Paul Klee

Klee, one of the great artist colourists of the 20th century, felt unified with colour. For him there were no arbitrary boundaries between his body and the world of colour he observed; he took it into his being, made it one with his self. You can tell by his words that colour was as necessary to him as breathing. Have you used colour with this same intensity? Now is the time to explore.

Look at any drawings you have done, including those you did for the 'Picture the Scene' visualization in the previous chapter. Have you used mainly the three primary colours? Red, yellow and blue shout out; they can't be missed because they demand attention with their exuberant energy.

Or have you used less emphatic colours? Orange, green and purple can be vivid, but may represent more subtle emotions. A blend of these colours can indicate more complicated, subtle or ambivalent feelings.

Ask yourself what the colours in your drawings are saying about your life at present. What 'temperature range' have you chosen? Remember, warm tones are reds and oranges, whilst blues and greens indicate the cool or cold end of the emotional range. Let's go further.

1 ***Have you used more warm colours?***	Warm colours reflect warmer feelings, a more energetic approach to life, and more passion or desire. But an excessive use of warm colours could mean anger.
2 ***Have you used more cool colours?***	Cool colours represent a calmer, more detached approach. They indicate a more thoughtful, reasoned way of being. But are you perhaps more passive than you want to be?
3 ***Have you coloured someone/something in cool colours when you thought you felt warmly towards them?***	If so, look again at this relationship. Is it what you want it to be? Are changes called for? Have you been feeling 'frozen out'?
4 ***Have you coloured someone/something in warm colours when you thought you felt coolly towards them?***	If so, reflect on your feelings. Is the choice of colour perhaps closer to your deeper attitude? Maybe you need to re-assess the situation. Are things 'hotting up'?

5 *Have you used pale pastels or ethereal colours?*	This use of colour indicates subtlety and sensitivity. But it may also show a passive attitude or lack of energy. Are you feeling overwhelmed at present? Do you need to re-charge your batteries? Are you a 'shadow of your former self' and feeling pale?
6 *Are there strong colour contrasts?*	Strong contrasts may indicate conflicts or contradictions in your life. Does this reflect concerns about relationships or inner turmoil about your path in life? Or is it that you prefer the ups and downs of life?
7 *How much space is there which has not been filled in?*	Lots of blank space can indicate emptiness. If you have included yourself in the picture, have you kept much space around you? If so, are you feeling cut off from other people? Or does it reflect a joy in individuality and a need for your own space?
8 *Is the overall mood of the scene bright and energetic?*	If it is, this shows a positive approach to life at present. But if it seems too busy, ask yourself if you're feeling stressed or out of control.
9 *Are the colours vivid?*	Vivid colours reflect strong feelings, exuberance, high energy levels, intensity and a direct, straightforward approach.
10 *Is the overall mood dull, muddy or unclear?*	If so, this would perhaps reflect a need for more clarity and definition in your life. Take some time to define your goals. What do you need to do to express your true potential? Working through 'Sifting for Gold' would be a good place to start!

Mandala

Mandalas, from the Hindu term for circle, are found throughout the East and symbolize the evolution of the soul from the biological to the spiritual world. Their intricate, usually circular designs are widely used to aid contemplation and visualization. You can find mandalas illustrated in many books or you can make your own and colour it in a way which you feel would enhance your creativity. You will benefit too from the vibrational energies of the colours which flow into you as you work.

As you colour your mandala, reflect on the qualities of the colours which you have read about in this book and affirm their positive power in your life.

I bring into my being the warmth of red.
I bring into my being the clarity of blue.
I bring into my being the wisdom of yellow.
I bring into my being the purity of white.
I bring into my being the majesty of purple.
I bring into my being the natural elements of green.

Now make up your own list.

Gaining Self-knowledge

Inscribed above the door of the temple at Delphi are the words 'Know Thyself'. This was the message of Apollo, the god of light and consciousness – the enlightened one. The journeys you have been taking in *Creative Visualization with Colour* are a colourful vision quest, a pilgrimage into your own centre.

Creative colour visualization using the golden rays of the sun will help illuminate your journey to enlightenment. The sprouting shoots of seeds remain in darkness until they are strong enough to make their way into the light. Perhaps there are aspects of you that are not yet ready for exposure. Perhaps you are 'in the dark' about parts of your nature, facets of yourself which have not yet appeared. This creative colour process will help you know yourself better.

A Creative Visualization of Yourself

Complete the following sentences and remember, spontaneity is the key. Using your notebook, write in as much detail as you want to. There is no right or wrong way; whatever you do is exactly right for you, so keep your critical censor out of the way. This process will provide you with nuggets of insight, true gold for you to treasure.

If I were a kind of *weather*, I would be/have . . .

If I were a *sky*, my colour would be . . .

If I were a *flower*, I would be . . .

If I were a *house*, I would be . . .

If I were an *animal*, I would be . . .

If my relationship with my mother and/or father were a *garden*, it would be . . .

If my whole life were a *path*, it would . . .

If my work were a *hill*, it would . . .

If I were in a pool with my friends, the *water* would be . . .

If I could *smell* of anything I want, I would choose . . .

If I were a *touch*, other people would feel . . .

Sifting through

Now look back at your responses. Go through them one at a time using the guide below to help. You may see an overall pattern or a range of complete opposites. What can you learn about yourself? Use further colour visualizations if you want more answers. If you find there is an aspect of yourself which you want to strengthen, go back to the colour which has the quality you need to develop and repeat the visualization, asking for help in the relevant area.

Weather You may have included some of the following words and phrases: 'storm tossed', 'damp', 'relentless driving rain', 'thundery', 'a face like thunder', 'a face like a wet weekend', 'a sunny disposition,' 'bright and cheerful', 'misty', 'foggy', 'cloudy', 'clouded vision', 'under the weather'. Consider how these weather images apply to your frame of mind. If you have chosen mainly cold images you could do more yellow colour visualizations to lift you to sunnier climes.

Sky Is the colour you chose for the sky bright or dull? Is it clear or cloudy? What are the characteristics of the colour and how does this reflect your emotions now?

Flower What flower did you choose? Is it smooth or spiky? What colour is it and what is this colour good for in terms of mind, body and spirit? Can you make any links with mythology; for example, roses symbolize love, lilies are often associated with death. Try to work out the symbolic significance of your flower. Has anyone ever given you this flower? If so, why might that be important to you at this point in your life?

House Is your house new or old? Is it well maintained and freshly decorated or is it run-down and in need of some attention? Is it grand or more modest? The state of the house may well reflect your present physical condition. If the windows and walls are damaged then you may be physically vulnerable at present. Consider each aspect of your house and ask yourself what it tells you about your present state of health. A blue healing and protection visualization will strengthen your immune system.

Animal Is your chosen animal wild or tamed and domesticated? Which words are usually associated with it: for example, strong (lion), cunning (fox), sensuous (cat), devoted (dog) or timid (gazelle)? How does this animal protect itself? Do you do the same? What can you learn from your chosen animal?

Garden How does your garden grow? Are the plants and trees blooming and fully grown? Do they have all they need to ensure healthy development? Are they native to your country or exotic imported plants? Do they reflect your personal development at this time? Visualize a seed growing from black earth to full bloom in glorious sunshine if you need a sense of renewal.

Path Is your path smooth and well worn? Or is it rocky, badly signposted and leading nowhere? Does it start off low but reach high plateaus? Is it straightforward or does it deviate and have many branches? What is your path in life? What direction are you travelling in? Are you a pathfinder, a trail blazer who leads the way? If your present path is unrewarding, a green colour visualization will help you to explore new avenues.

Hill Is your hill fertile or sterile, bleak or filled with birds and wildlife? Is it inviting? Often hills symbolize struggles in life so their size and your feelings about them will give you clues to your present situation. A hill often represents aspirations – emotional, physical or spiritual – and achievements to be followed up, goals to be reached. Is your hill formidable, filling you with fear, or do you think you could climb it if you wanted to? Visualize a strong guide who will help you climb if you need extra strength or support.

Water The quality of the water, whether it is clear, muddy, teeming with life or sterile, gives you clues. Is your pool deep, warm and inviting or is it shallow with sharp rocks? Are your friends happy to be 'in the swim' with you? Do you have any fears that you might 'go under'? What is the colour of the water? Go back to the appropriate colour chapter if you need more information to decipher your pool communication. A visualization with red and orange will give you increased energy to develop new friendships or to sustain more long-standing ones.

Smell Is it pleasant or pungent? A natural smell of roses, pine woods or lavender? Or have you chosen a perfume bought from a shop? Is the smell masculine or feminine? Explore the potential of aromatherapy oils. They can be a real bonus to colour visualization.

Touch Would you feel leathery, well worn and a bit dried out, or would you be soft, smooth and warm? Are you 'prickly' and easily ruffled? Does water 'run off your back' or are you thin skinned, transparent and easily upset? The touch you choose tells you about the impression you want to make on other people. Fear makes your outer layer (emotionally speaking), tougher and harder to penetrate. If you want to be more open, try a visualisation with green and pink so you can have safe, healing, unconditional love and growth.

Colour Yourself in

On a piece of paper or in your notebook, write the answers to these questions.

What colours are you wearing right now?
What does your choice say about you?
What colours do you usually wear?
What colours don't you wear?
What impression does your colour choice make on other people?
What impression would you like to make on people?
What colours could you choose?

Have a look through the clothes in your wardrobe if you are not sure about your preferences. Make a note of any changes you would like to make. Remember, you don't need to buy a whole new wardrobe; you can add splashes of colour with scarves, accessories and simple jewellery.

Creative Visualization with your Favourite Colour

You will need some paper and a pen for this visualization so have them ready before you continue. An alarm clock too! You can do this with a trusted friend or alone.

Follow the relaxation routine on pages 23–5 and when you feel fully relaxed, think about your favourite colour; imagine it in all its shades and tones. Feel yourself in a place where this colour predominates. What can you see? What does it feel like to be embraced by your colour? Do this for just a couple of minutes then open your eyes. On the piece of paper you have in front of you, write the name of your chosen colour at the top. Then set the alarm clock for seven minutes and begin to write.

What you are aiming for is spontaneous creative writing, like a visualization with written words. The guidelines are simple.

1 Write whatever comes into your head.
2 Do not allow your critical censor to interfere: don't listen to your inner voice saying 'I can't write that, it's stupid'; 'It won't make sense'; 'It's too embarrassing'. Forget all that, just let your creativity flow.
3 Remember that whatever you write is right.
4 Don't stop writing even if it's 'I'm stuck, I don't know what to write next'. Just write all your thoughts down.

5 When the time is up, finish the phrase/sentence and put the time, date and place.
6 Finally, read through your piece and underline the words or phrases which you find most interesting, surprising or descriptive, or which you just love!

Whatever you have written has come from your unconscious mind and is therefore telling you something about yourself. It may refer to important connections you need to make, it may have given the sensitivity of your vision an outlet, or it may have put you in touch with collective myths you share with others from places and cultures far away in time and space.

Now go through what you have written and consider these questions:

1 What was the general feeling about your colour? Was it happy, sad, reflective, joyous, angry, energetic, nostalgic, etc?
2 What things did you include? Were they natural – people, animals, trees, etc – or man-made – roads, buildings, vehicles, etc?
3 Was the tone of the writing cool or warm? Does this reflect your mood at present?
4 Did your writing refer to past events in your life? If so, what importance do they still hold for you?
5 What light does your writing throw on your present life? What does it say to you?

You may find it helpful to read about Zoe's experience.

Zoe's surprise

During one creative visualization journey, run as part of a stress management course, I asked participants to receive a gift for themselves. One person received a ring, another a teddy bear, and a third was given a statue. There was a wide variety of responses, as there always is. In the discussion that completed the exercise, not all present wanted to share their journey with the group. A few days later, I received this letter from Zoe, which shows just how healing creative visualization with colour can be. She wrote,

> **I went along a path, actually felt the grass beneath my feet, and went down to a beach. I was on the beach in every sense, sand between my toes, sound of the waves and seagulls high above me.**

> I looked up and in the distance saw a high cliff. There was someone in a mist on the cliff edge; I expected that person to be my husband, but as the mist cleared it wasn't, it was my mum.
>
> At this point I didn't want to carry on. I opened my eyes and really wanted to escape the room but because I knew that if I did I would more than likely disrupt everyone else's journey, I decided to stay and keep quiet until everyone had returned.
>
> Before I knew what was happening, I was back on the beach looking up and my mum gave me the gift, which was a box wrapped in blue shiny paper, with thin white ribbon round it and a label.

She explained the background to all that she had experienced.

> My mum died in hospital two years ago this month after being unconscious for five weeks. I am an only child. We spoke most days on the phone and she spent large chunks of time at our house, because when she was not with us she was very lonely. One day, someone at work was selling gifts for cancer research and I bought one for my mum. These gifts were empty boxes, gift wrapped with a ribbon and label. I can't remember the exact words on the label, but they were to this effect: 'This gift is from me to you; when you are feeling lonely and blue, just touch the gift and you'll feel my love for you'.
>
> Whilst she was in hospital, I took the gift box and left it on her locker, but when she died, the box got mislaid and I have never thought about it since.

Zoe's mother never fully regained consciousness but from time to time she recognized people and spoke to them, but never to Zoe.

> This obviously upset me a great deal. And, as you can imagine, for me the visualization was very emotional. It came as quite a shock.

But it brought Zoe a great deal of unexpected comfort. She thanked me for providing the opportunity to make the healing contact that her visualization brought. The blue and silver parcel reflects the feminine silver of the moon and the loyalty and devotion of blue. You may recall that blue is the colour associated with motherly love and this connection was clearly so for Zoe.

Time to reflect

Take time to look back at your visualizations. Do you feel they were healing in any way? Also, what affirmations did you receive? If you are unclear about whether you got any at all, then try this next activity. And even if you are clear, you might like to do this anyway, so have a go. Many of us have lost touch with our creative powers and wonder if we can ever access them again. The answer is that you can and this is to help you do just that.

Active Colour Meditation

Collect together coloured pencils, paints and paper. You are about to start an active colour meditation. It releases right-brain creativity and allows the colours' vibrations to energize you as you work.

First decide which colour you need at the present moment. Then gather together a selection of items in various shades and tints of this colour. You could collect leaves, petals, stones and so on as well as objects you have about your home. If you chose green, for example, you could cover a small table or flat area with a green cloth. On it you might place a green plant, a green gemstone, a green candle, some grasses and any other objects or pictures which would help with your visualization and spiritual practice.

Now sit in front of the arrangement you have made. Breathe in the colour and allow it to fill your senses. When you are ready to start, draw or paint it. Try to capture the feelings you have rather than faithfully try to make a realistic rendition. If you find that you want to paint a seemingly unconnected image, that's fine. Go with the flow and let your creative imagination take the lead.

Once you have completed your picture, leave it and go back to it later to discover its message to you. Write down your responses as affirmations; here is one to start you off.

- Every person is a shining link in the chain of my wellbeing.

Make your Desires a Reality

In the visualization of your perfect living space (see page 113) there were a number of questions to help you identify what you wanted. Looking back at the notes you made, take some time to consider what you can do to make those desires a reality.

As you know, visualizations are part of a creative process that can bring change into your life. Once you have thought about what you want then make the thoughts more concrete by going through this 'actualization exercise', which I developed from an excellent one in Jane Alexander's *Spirit of the Home*.

Home Sweet Home Actualization

On a large sheet of paper, paint the colour of your perfect home. It does not have to be an actual colour that you want to paint the walls, but make it a colour that captures the feel you want your home to have. If you cannot decide, then paint your sheet gold or pinky-gold. Gold attracts good things and pinky-gold brings gentle healing.

When you have done that, get a photograph of yourself and stick it in the middle of the paper. You are at the centre of this process just as you are the centre of your home. Now write words on the paper or stick on pictures from magazines or photographs you have taken. Gradually you are defining and creating the space you want. Use your notes so you can include the insight you gained from your Hestia visualization (page 113).

When you have stuck on all that you want, including perhaps some symbols of the roles you would like to have in your home – lover, parent, artist, chef – place the picture in a spot where you will see it every day. This could be on a notice board, for example, or in a drawer you open each day or by your bedside. Whenever you see the picture make an affirmation.

- My wonderful space is ready and waiting for me.

Through the host of creative visualizations with colour which you have experienced in this book, you have discovered elements of your nature which may have been hidden or repressed for a long time. As they now become part of your everday life, treat them gently, nourish them and use your nuggets of gold to help you each and every day. In this final section you put together all those insights and affirm your path of abundance in mind, body and spirit.

Your Personal Action Plan

Your collection of notes on your colour visualizations as well as your creative colour writings and paintings, provide vital information about how you are living your life and about the direction of your journey in life. Wherever you are on this path, now is the most precious time you have. Cherish it as you consider what you would like to do in future.

Now, with heartfelt kindness to yourself, make a personal action plan to help you on your way. See it as a sturdy rucksack containing all the essentials you need for your mind, body and spirit.

Colour qualities

I am going to have more .... (colour) in my life.
I will include it by ....
(Think of food, clothes, paintings, flowers, gemstones and so on.)

Loving kindness

The gift I received/would have liked to receive was ....
The gift has helped me to understand that ....
To show more loving kindness to myself I ....
To show more loving kindness to others I ....

The re-enchantment of my home

To nurture myself at home I will ....
To honour my place in the wider world which is also my home
I will ....

The crown of creativity

All I produce is unique and of value. To sustain my creativity I will ....

New beginnings

Having experienced the colour visualizations, I will take the knowledge and use it to loosen bonds with people and things that are harmful to me and I will build new, healthier ones. I can do this in the following ways:

1 ....
2 ....
3 ....

Affirmations to help me every day

1 ....
2 ....
3 ....

Go back through the book and write in affirmations that you particularly liked, or make up your own.

Your journey to this point is full of nuggets of gold; some may already be visible, others are still hidden, waiting to be discovered as you explore another seam of your life.

Cherish the moment you have. Celebrate your essence now and be open to all that awaits you.

Go in Love and Peace.

Further Reading

Alexander, Jane, *Spirit of the Home*, Thorsons, London, 1998

Allanach, Jack, *Colour Me Healing*, Element, Shaftesbury, 1997

Birren, Faber, *The Symbolism of Colour*, Carol Publishing, New York, 1989

Birren, Faber, 'The Practical Application of Light and Colour to Human Environments', International Color Association, 2nd Congress, Adam Hilger, London, 1973

Cirlot, J E, *A Dictionary of Symbols*, Routledge & Kegan Paul, London, 1962

Connell, Camilla, *Something Understood*, Art Books International, London, 1998

Cousins, Norman, *An Anatomy of Illness*, Bantam Books, London, 1986

Cowan, James G, *The Aborigine Tradition*, Element, Shaftesbury, 1992

Dalichow, Irene, and Booth, Mike, *Aura-Soma: Healing Through Color, Plant and Crystal Energy*, Hay House Publications, USA, 1996

Gawain, Shakti, *Creative Visualization*, New World Library, California, 1995

Gimbel, Theo, *Healing With Colour*, Gaia Books, London, 1994

Goldstein, Kurt, 'Some experimental observations concerning the influence of colour on the function of an organism', *Occupational Therapy and Rehabilitation*, June 1942

Growning, Karl, *Decorated Skin: A World Survey of Body Art*, Thames & Hudson, London, 1997

Herbert, Marie, *Healing Quest*, Rider, Random House, London, 1996

Hill, Justina, *Germs and Man*, G P Putnam, New York, 1940

Holford, Patrick, *The Optimum Nutrition Bible*, Piatkus, London, 1998

Hope, Augustine, and Walch, Margaret, *Colour Compedium*, Van Nostrand Reinhold, New York, 1990

Hunt, R, *The Seven Keys of Colour Healing*, C W Daniel, Saffron Walden, 1968

Hurvich, L M, *Colour Vision*, Sinauer Associates, Sunderland, Mass, 1981

Kabat-Zinn, J, *Full Catastrophe Living*, Dell Publishing, New York 1991

Kaiser, P K, and Boynton, R M, *Human Colour Vision*, Optical Society of America, Washington DC, 1996

Kubler-Ross, Dr E, *To Live Until We Say Goodbye*, Prentice-Hall, 1978

Itten J, *The Art of Colour*, Reinhold, New York, 1961

Lazenby, Gina, *The Feng Shui House Book*, Conran Octopus, London, 1997

Levine, Stephen, *Who Dies?*, Gateway Books, Bath, 1986

Low, Albert, *Feng Shui: The Way to Harmony*, Pelanduk Publications, Weatherhill, 1998

Mallon, Brenda, *Helping Children To Manage Loss: Strategies for Renewal and Growth*, Jessica Kingsley, London, 1998

Mallon, Brenda, *Women Dreaming*, Fontana, London, 1987

Moen, Larry, *Meditations For Awakening*, United States Publishing, Hawaii, 1994

Pope, Sandra and Nori, *Colour By Design*, Conran Octopus, London, 1998

Roosbach, Susan, *Interior Design*, Penguin, London, 1987

Sargent, Walter, *The Enjoyment and Use of Colour*, Dover, New York, 1964

Siegel, Dr Bernie, *Love, Medicine & Miracles*, Arrow, London, 1986

Simpson, Liz, *The Book of Crystal Healing*, Gaia Books, London, 1997

Verner-Bonds, Lilian, *Colour Healing*, Vermillion, London, 1994

Verner-Bonds, Lilian, and Corvo, Joseph, *The Healing Power of Colour Zone Therapy*, Piatkus, London, 1997

Walker, Barbara G, *A Woman's Dictionary of Symbols and Sacred Objects*, Harper SanFrancisco, 1988

Wandell, B, *Foundations of Vision*, Sinauer Associates, USA, 1995

Wills, Pauline, *The Reflexology and Colour Therapy Workbook*, Element, Shaftesbury, 1992

Wills, Pauline, *Colour Therapy*, Element, Shaftesbury, 1993

Ulrich, Robert, 'Effects of Interior Design on Wellness: Theory and Recent Scientific Resarch', *Journal of Health Care Interior Design*, 1991

Grateful thanks are given for permission to quote from the following works:

John Ruskin: The Early Years, 1819–1859, Tim Hilton (ed), Yale University Press; *Marc Chagall*, by Sidney Alexander, Cassell, London; *Nansen*, by Roland Huntford, Duckworth Press, London; 'Postscript' from *The Spirit Level*, by Seamus Heaney, Faber and Faber, London; *Who Dies?*, by Steven Levine, Gateway Publishers, Bath; *The Healing Power of Colour Zone Therapy*, by Joseph Corvo and Lilian Verner Bonds, Piatkus Books, London; *The Seagull*, Michael Frayn (trans), Methuen, London; *Vincent van Gogh*, by James Lassaigne, Thames and Hudson, London; *Meditations for Awakening*, by Larry Moen, United States Publishing, Hawaii; *Galileo and the Solar System*, by Paul Strathern, Arron Books, London.

All efforts have been made to trace authors who have been quoted, however this has not been possible in all cases. Please contact us to rectify any omission and accept our apologies.

Useful Addresses

EUROPE

Affiliation of Crystal Healing Organizations (ACHO)
46 Lower Green Road
Esher
Surrey KT10 8HD
UK
Tel: 0181 398 7252

British Register of Complementary Practitioners
PO Box 194
London SE16 1QZ
UK
(send large SAE)
Tel: 0171 237 6175

Colour Therapy Association
PO Box 16756
London SW20 8ZW
UK
Tel: 0181 540 3540

Hygeia College of Colour Therapy
Brook House
Avening
Tetbury
Glos GL8 8NS
UK
Tel: 01453 832150

The International Association for Colour Therapy (IACT)
PO Box 3
Potters Bar
Herts EN6 3ET
UK

The Institute for Complementary Medicine
Unit 5, Tavern Quay
Commercial Centre
Rope Street
London SE16 1TX
UK

Brenda Mallon
Creative Therapies
7 Didsbury Park
Didsbury
Manchester M20 5HL
Tel: 0161 448 8780
Fax: 0161 448 2269
E-mail: lapwing@gn.apc.org

Margaret Warbrick
Aura-Soma practitioner and image consultant
Cranford Court
King Street
Knutsford
Cheshire WA16 8BW
UK
Tel: 01565 652 616

Pauline Wills
The Oracle School of Colour
9 Wyndale Avenue
Kingsbury
London NW9 9PT
UK
Tel: 0181 204 7672

USA

American Holistic Medical Association
Suite 201
4101 Lake Boone Trail
Raleigh
NC 27607
Tel: 919 787 5181

Aura-Soma USA Inc
PO Box 1688
Canyon Lake
TX 78130
Tel: 210 935 2355

Judith Cornell PhD
Manifesting Inner Light
PO Box 517
Sausalito
CA 94966–0517
Tel: 415 332 4663
E-mail: ommandala@aol.com

Shakti Gawain
PO Box 377
Mill Valley
CA 94942

Index

Abundance 62, 67, 72, 124, 142
Acupuncture 13, 47
Addiction 89
Affirmations 3, 4, 23, 33, 39, 49, 50, 55, 62, 67, 78, 83, 88, 89, 92, 102, 104, 110–11, 115, 121–3, 140–1, 143
Anger 6, 9, 14, 29, 98
Anaemia 10, 30, 74
Animals 8, 9, 17, 68, 69, 97, 122, 126, 134–5
Anorexia 37, 73
Antioxidants 32
Anxiety 14, 24, 30
Art therapy 98
Arthritis 46, 74, 126
Atlantis 15
Aura 14, 15, 33, 47, 125
Aura-Soma 12, 16
Asthma 10
Ayurvedic medicine 16

Baba Ram Dass 27
Bereavement 37
Birren, Faber 30, 43
Black 11, 13, 96–102, 105, 123–4, 135
Blood 28, 30, 31, 33, 38, 46, 75, 89
Blood pressure 10, 11, 12, 20, 21, 31, 45, 64, 74
Blue 9–11, 17– 20, 33, 40–57, 85, 86, 87, 93, 94, 108, 120, 121, 123, 131, 133, 139
Brain 2, 5, 9, 12, 31, 130
Brown 17, 61, 102, 105
Buddha 11, 28, 66, 71

Cancer 6, 20, 32, 98, 139
Celtic 44
Chakras 10, 11, 13–17, 30, 31, 33, 36, 37, 44, 45, 53, 58, 59, 66, 72, 73, 81, 85, 92–5, 102, 116, 120, 127
China 31, 45, 71, 74, 94, 127
'Colour Me Beautiful' 18
Colour Therapy 8–11, 14, 15, 17, 37, 54, 59, 74
Colour visualization 5, 20, 21, 79–81, 86, 87, 108, 133, 134, 136, 142
Colour wheel 17, 18, 50
Complementary colours 11, 18, 19, 50, 58
Creative Visualization 1–8, 13, 19, 21–3, 25, 32, 38, 48, 51, 54, 59, 64, 68, 70, 75, 88, 101, 103, 109, 133, 137–8, 141
Creativity 1, 4, 5, 9, 11, 22, 27, 28, 31, 33, 36, 39, 46, 72, 104, 114, 124, 137, 140, 142
Crystals 15, 16, 21, 22, 30, 31, 37, 47, 64, 74, 87, 98, 116, 118–19, 121

Depression 6, 37, 74, 86, 97, 98, 100, 126
Diagnosis 9, 45
Disease 6, 7, 16, 20, 21
Divorce 37
Dreams 31, 51, 74, 98, 105, 114, 118

Egyptian 11, 27, 43, 44, 57–8, 99, 124, 126–7
Electromagnetic energy 10, 14, 15
Emotions 9, 12
Endocrine system 14, 53, 72, 116

Energy systems 9, 13, 14

Failure 7, 8
Feng Shui 12, 57
Fertility 12, 30, 31, 33, 103–4

Gemstones 11, 15, 16, 31, 37, 44, 47, 64, 74, 87, 118, 140
Gold 11, 35, 40, 55, 60, 62, 69, 71, 89, 102, 110, 123–32, 134, 140–1, 143
Greeks 3, 11, 28, 43, 72, 96, 127
Green 11, 12, 17–20, 22, 51, 56–70, 89, 95, 103–4, 108, 116, 120, 123, 131, 133, 136, 140
Grey 63, 101, 108
Grief 11, 88

Healing 6–10, 13, 15, 17, 30, 31, 32, 37, 46, 47, 53, 55, 59, 62–5, 70, 73, 74, 87, 86, 89, 91, 98, 108–9, 118, 126, 127, 135, 138–41
Health 6, 7, 10, 13, 15, 16, 17
Heart 20, 30, 31, 33, 37, 47, 57, 60, 62, 64, 66, 69, 70, 72, 74, 89, 102, 104, 105, 112, 113, 115
Heraldry 11, 28, 44, 85, 107
Herbert, Marie 53
Hindu 43
Hormones 6
Hospitals 12, 63

Illness 6, 8, 9, 15, 46, 63
Imagery 2, 25
Immune system 6, 7, 20, 21, 32, 55, 59, 135
India 97
Indigo 53, 60, 108, 116, 120, 123
Intuition 2, 5, 9, 22, 37, 55, 64, 71, 75
Inspiration 9, 43, 64, 71
Islam 11
Itten, Johannes 18

Jekyll, Gertrude 19
Judaism 11

Kidneys 30, 37
Kundalini 30

Lavender 87, 108, 114, 136
Lemon 74, 108
Light 8, 11, 15, 27, 46, 72, 97–8, 107, 133
Lilac 93, 94, 108
Limbic system 9
Liver 31
Love 6, 27, 31, 33, 37, 43, 47, 57, 58, 64, 71, 82, 94, 99, 107, 135–6

Magenta 58, 93, 95
Mandala 133
Meditation 47, 58, 63, 72, 85, 88, 118–19, 123, 140
Mental health 20
Mind–body 14
Monet 18
Moon 8, 37, 43, 104, 105

Nansen, Fridtjof 45
Native Americans 44, 53, 97, 118, 126, 127

Orange 11, 12, 17, 18, 20, 27, 29, 33, 35–9, 49, 55, 60, 75, 82, 83, 89, 108, 116, 120, 131, 136

Personal development 9, 55
Pink 20, 31, 35, 40, 41, 44, 66, 123, 136
Pineal gland 93
Pituitary gland 53
Problem solving 7, 9, 38
Protection 9
Positive Thinking 2, 5, 6, 31
Purple 11, 12, 19, 60, 84–95, 131, 133

Rainbow 8, 15, 27, 94, 108, 115–22, 126
Red 9–13, 18, 19, 26–40, 43, 45, 50,

51, 71–3, 85, 86, 93, 94, 98, 108, 116, 120, 122–3, 131, 133, 136
Relaxation 5, 9, 10, 23, 25, 54, 65, 109, 110
Reproduction 27
Rituals 4, 39, 57–8, 97
Ruskin John 43

Sanskrit 13, 28, 30, 81
Scott Fitzgerald, F 50
Seasonal Affective Disorder (SAD) 97–8
Self-confidence 4, 7, 18, 31, 37, 38, 86
Sexuality 27, 28, 30, 37
Silver 53, 95, 96, 100, 104–6, 127, 139
Spectrum 8, 10, 12, 14, 15, 16, 27, 44, 50, 57, 72, 93, 108, 116, 121
Spirit 10, 31, 42, 43, 44, 53, 85, 89, 91, 92, 94, 101, 110, 140
Stars 8, 38
Stress 7, 8, 20, 37, 45, 54, 75, 86, 87, 108
Suicide 12
Sun 8, 24, 28, 37, 40, 51, 60, 61, 73–5, 79, 83, 96, 103, 106, 116, 122, 124–6
Surgery 8, 86
Symbolism 11, 37, 39, 43, 46, 66, 70, 72, 94, 125, 128
Sympathetic magic 3, 58, 73, 97

Therapy 30
Thyroid 45, 64
Tones 19, 107–15
Trauma 37, 98
Turquoise 50, 51, 53–5

Van Gogh, Vincent 43–4, 71, 101
Vibrations 9, 10, 15, 16, 19, 20, 22, 64, 72, 87, 88, 93, 133, 140
Violet 11, 18, 50, 73, 93, 94, 108, 116, 120
Visualization 2, 19, 20, 22, 25, 33, 38, 45, 49, 62, 69, 73, 78, 80, 86, 89, 92–4, 100, 110–12, 118–19, 121, 124, 128, 131, 133, 135, 139–42

White 11, 12, 19, 28, 33, 40, 42, 43, 44, 51, 54, 63, 70, 71, 89, 92, 96, 99, 101, 105–10, 116, 119–21, 123, 133, 139

Yellow 11, 18, 36, 40, 43, 50, 51, 57, 70–9, 84, 85, 89, 108–9, 111, 116, 120, 126, 131, 133–4
Yoga 13, 85

5

Printed in the United States
29028LVS00001B/46

9 781843 331568